this celebration of anal belongs to:

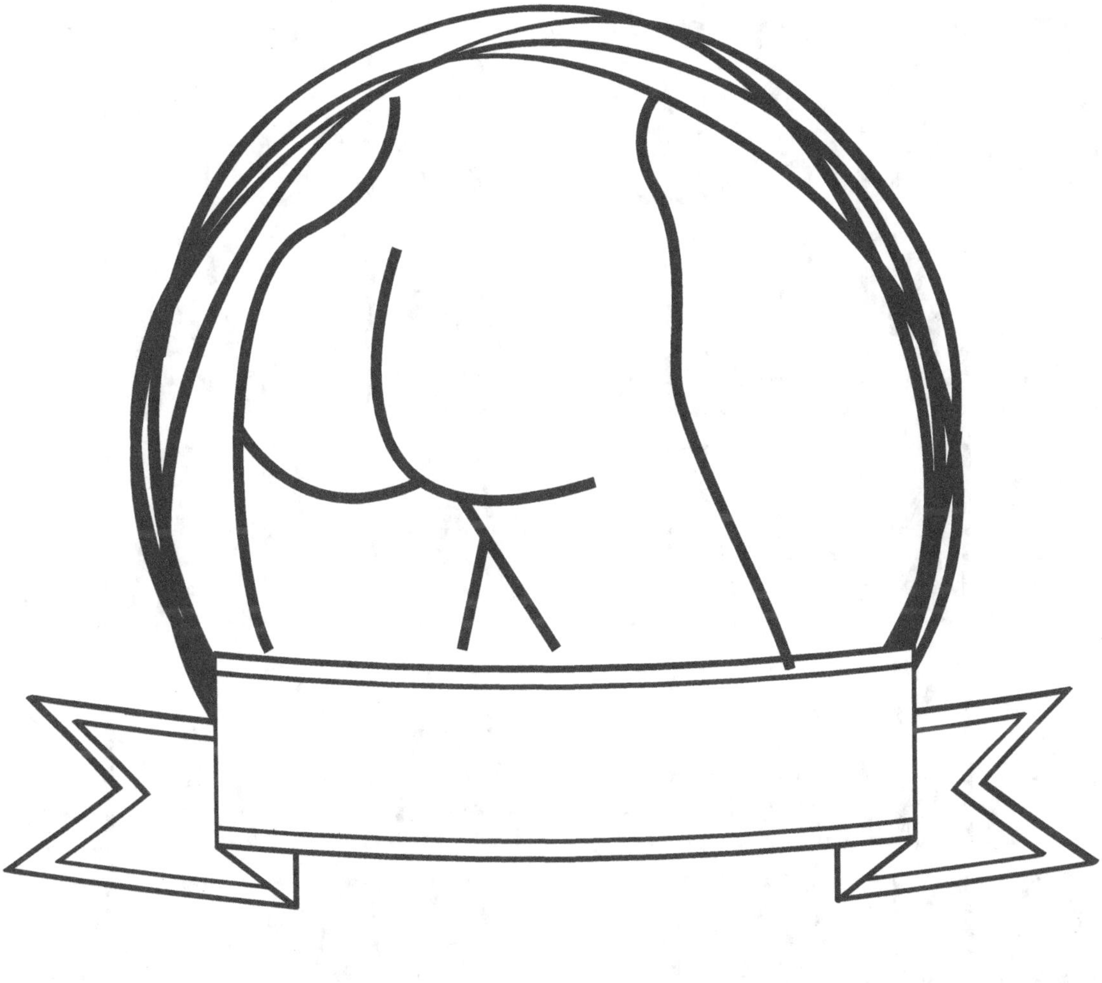

ANAL ANAL
ANAL ANAL
ANAL ANAL
ANAL ANAL
ANAL ANAL
ANAL ANAL

ANAL ANAL
ANAL ANAL
ANAL ANAL
ANAL ANAL
ANAL ANAL
ANAL ANAL

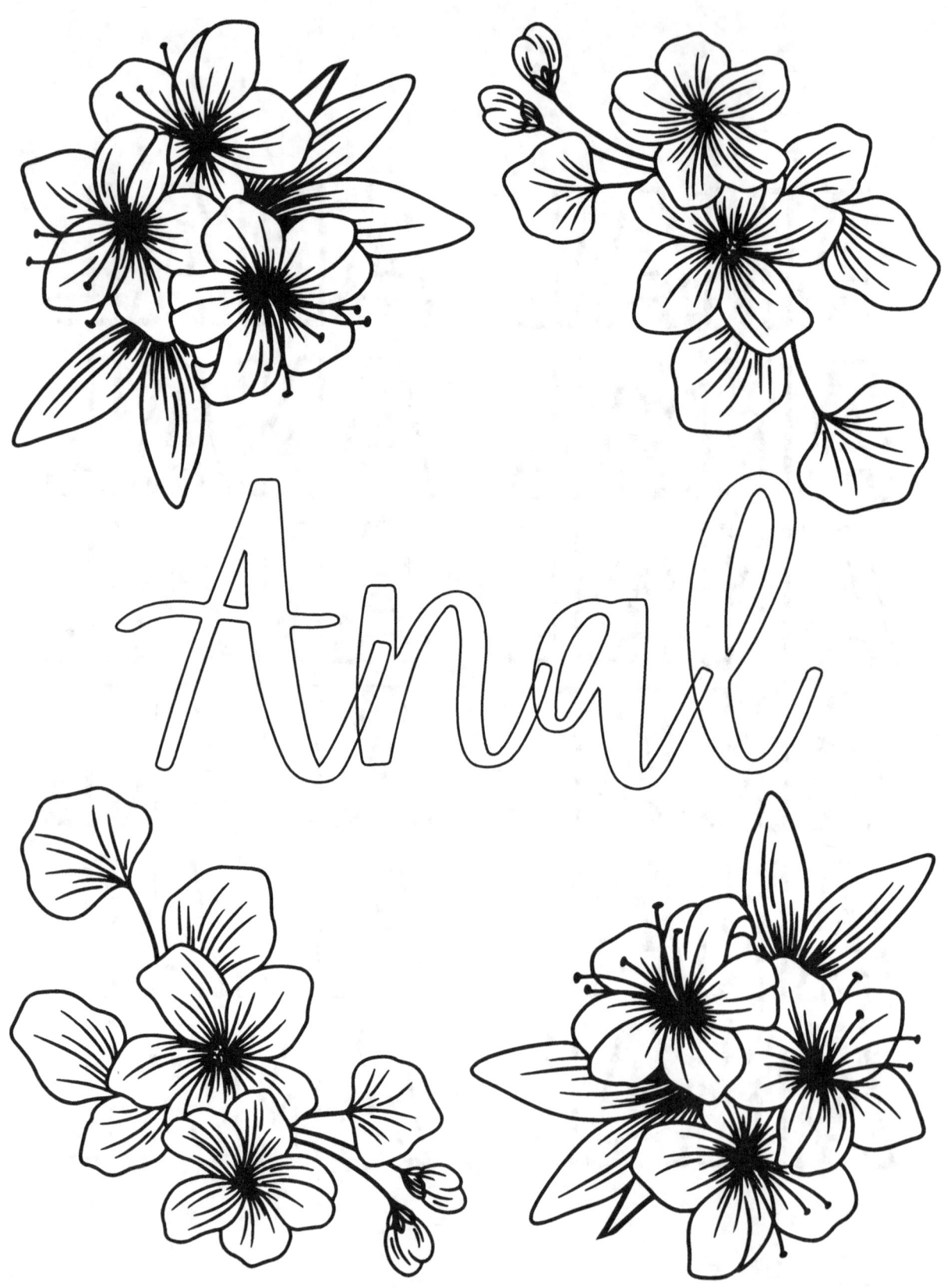

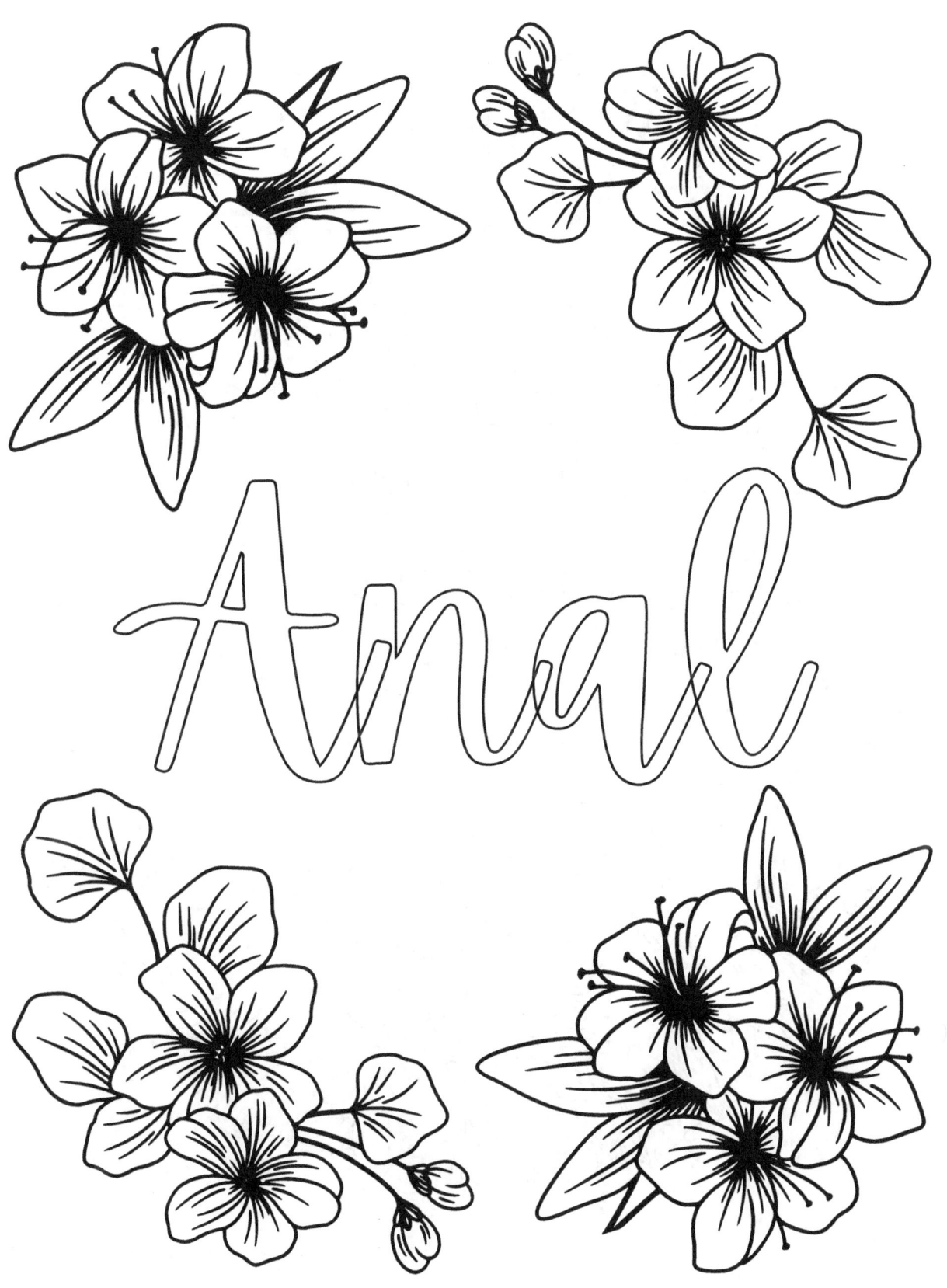

ANAL

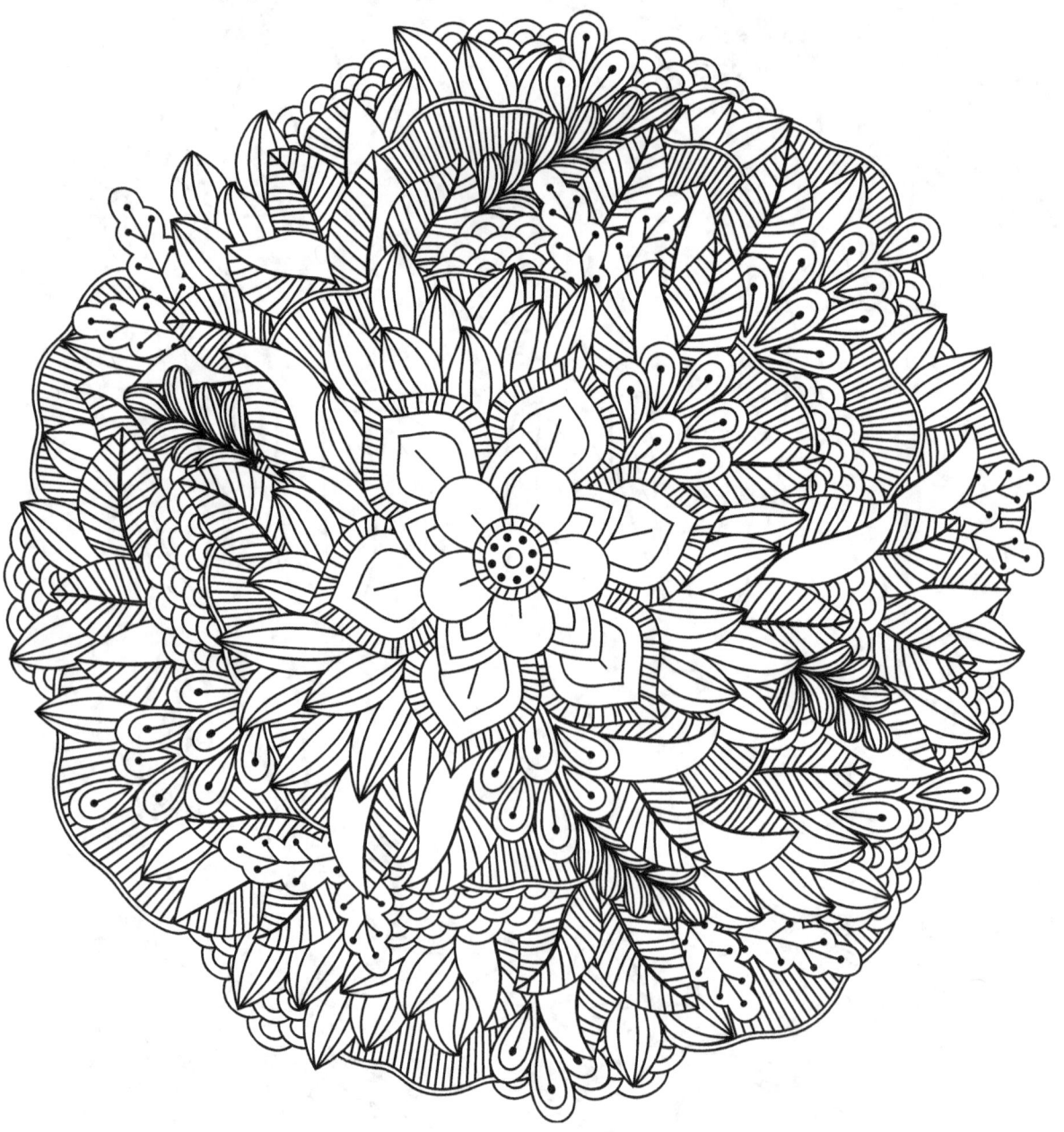

ANAL

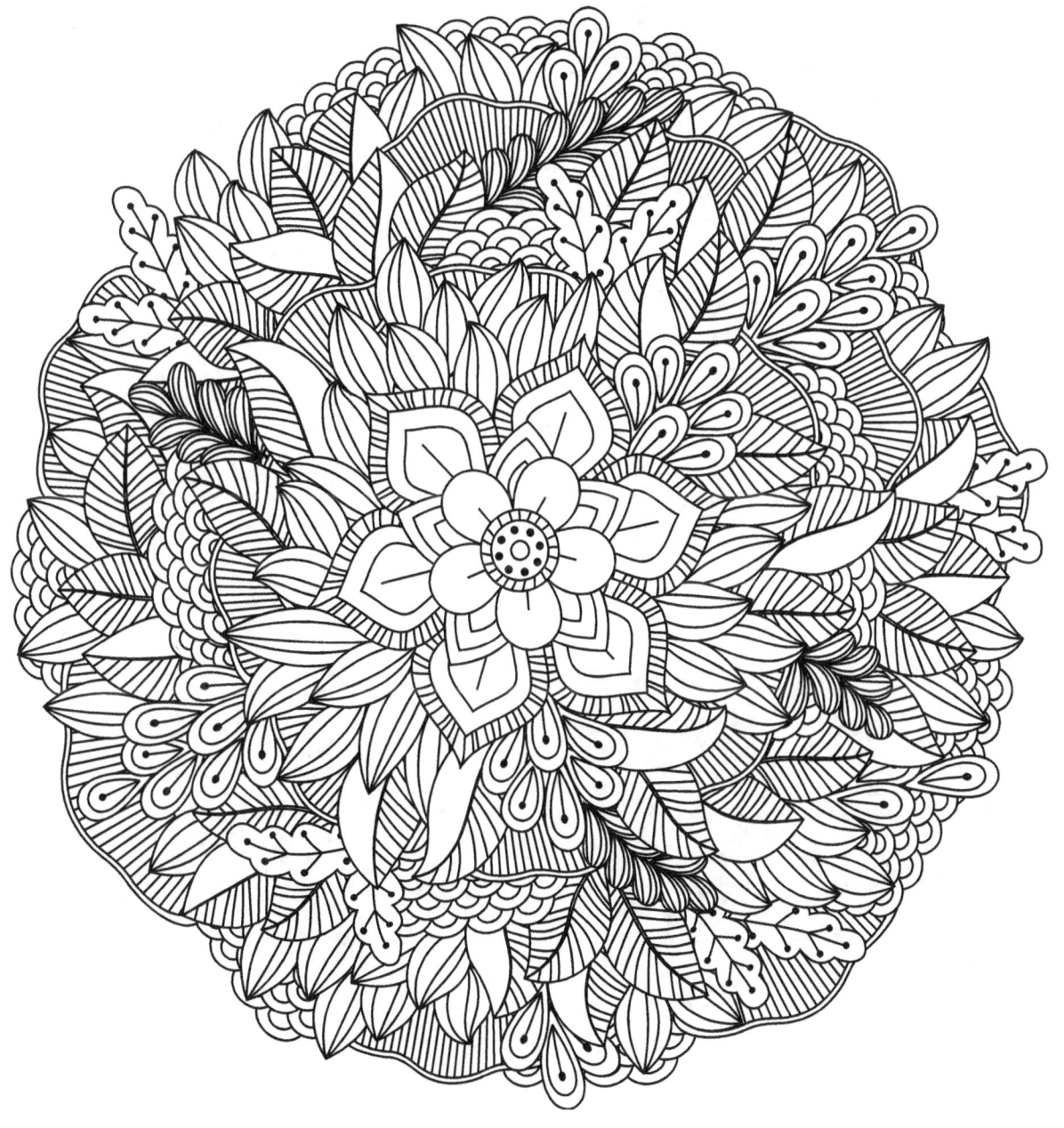

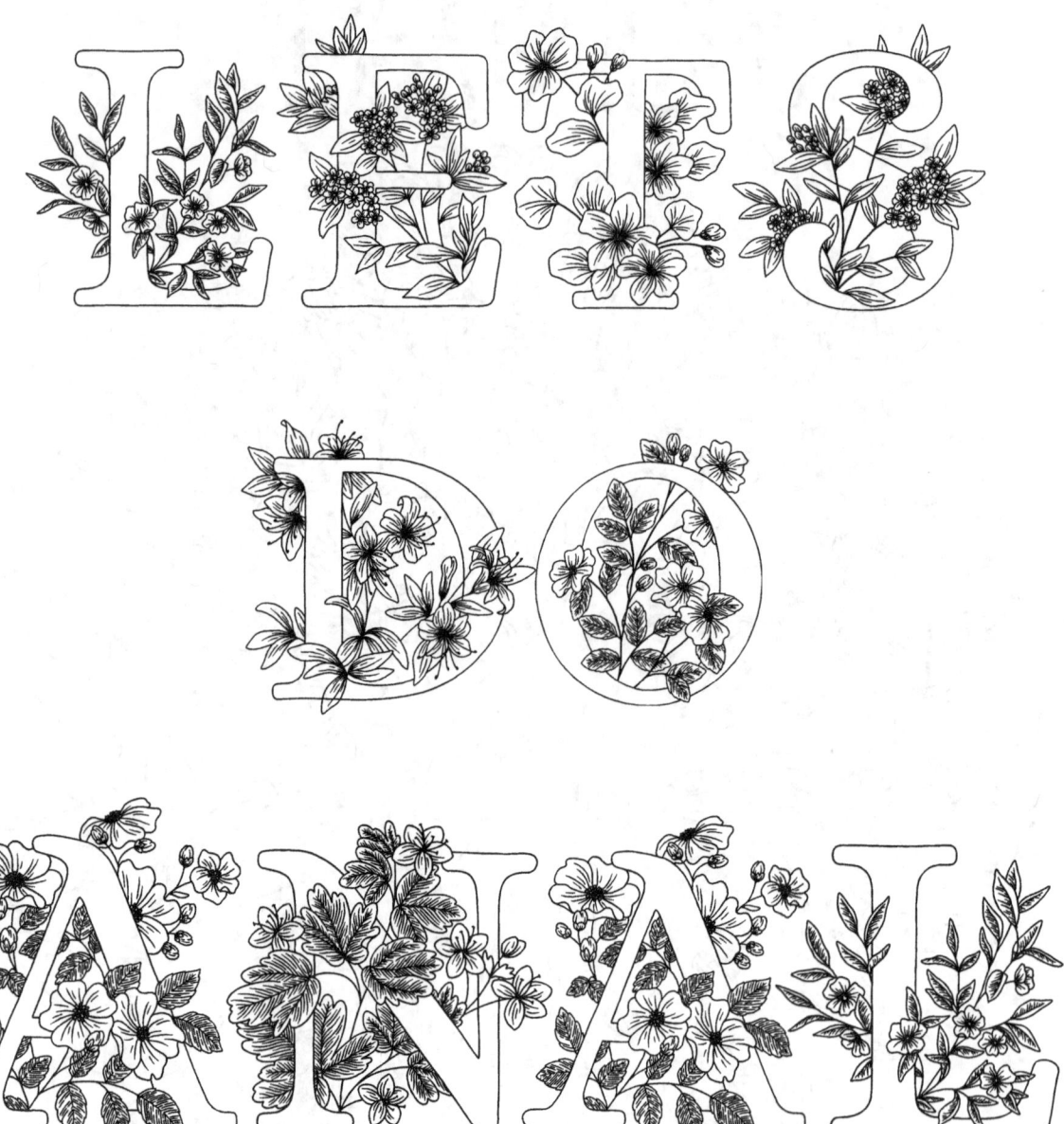

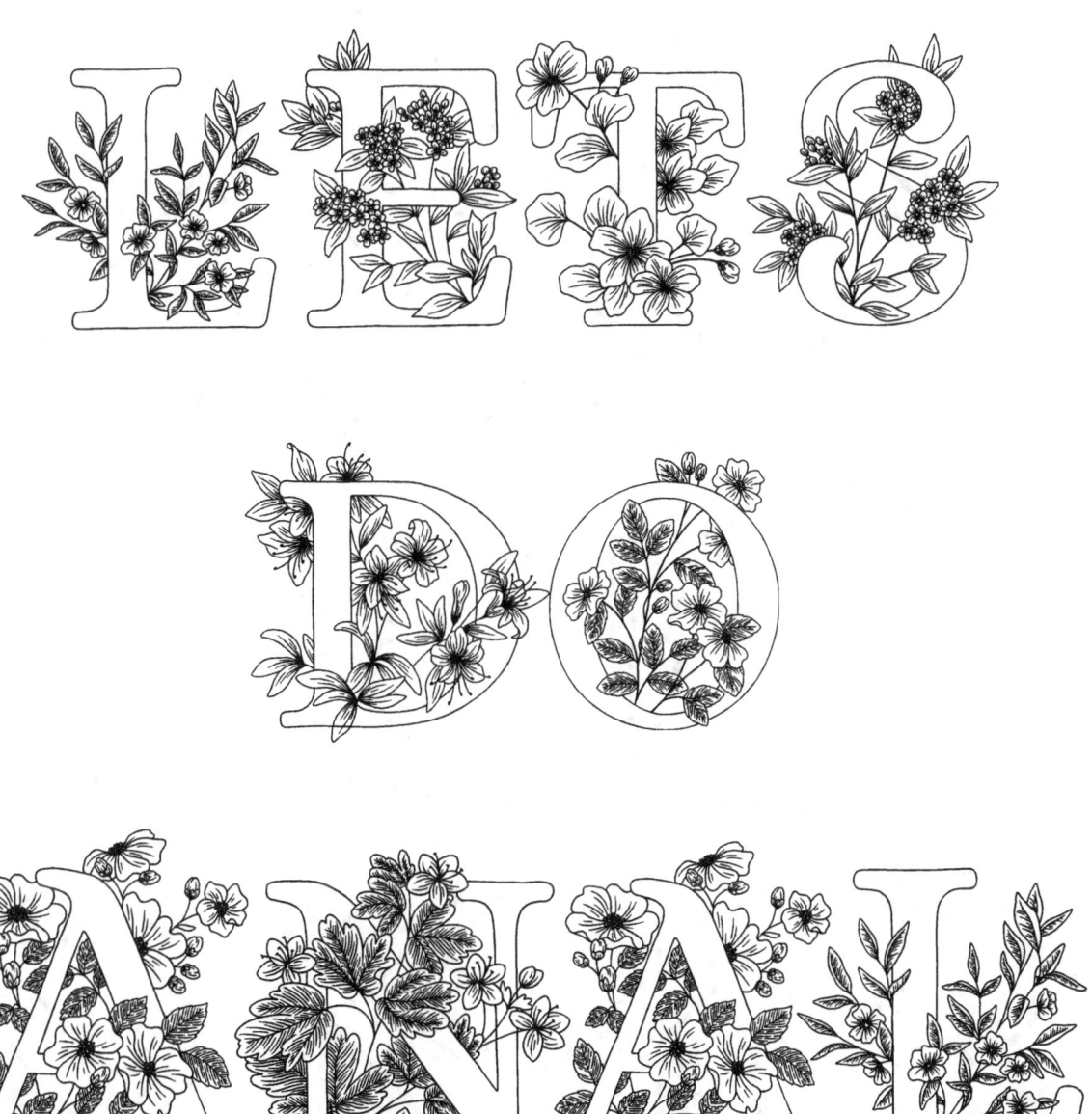

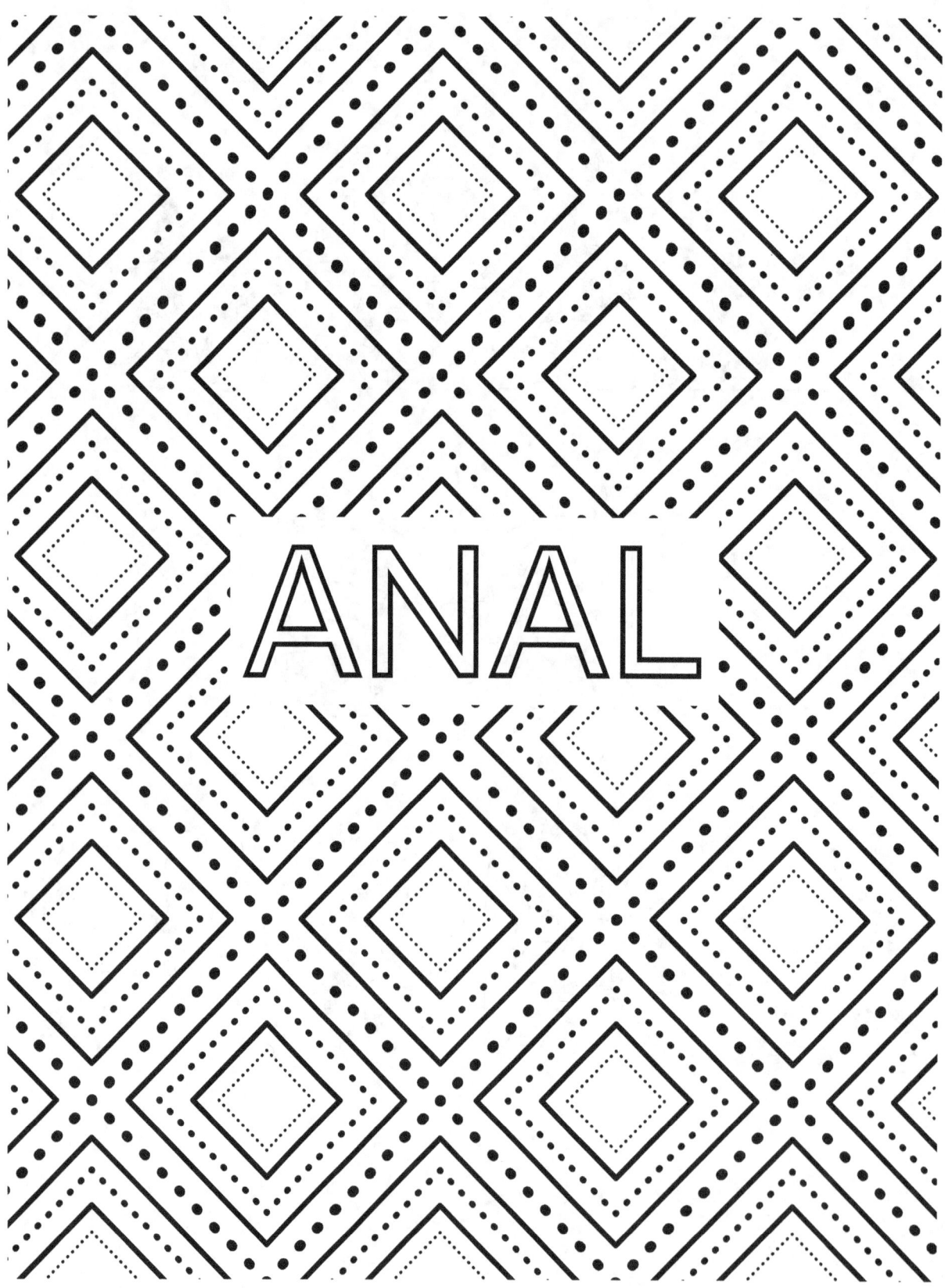

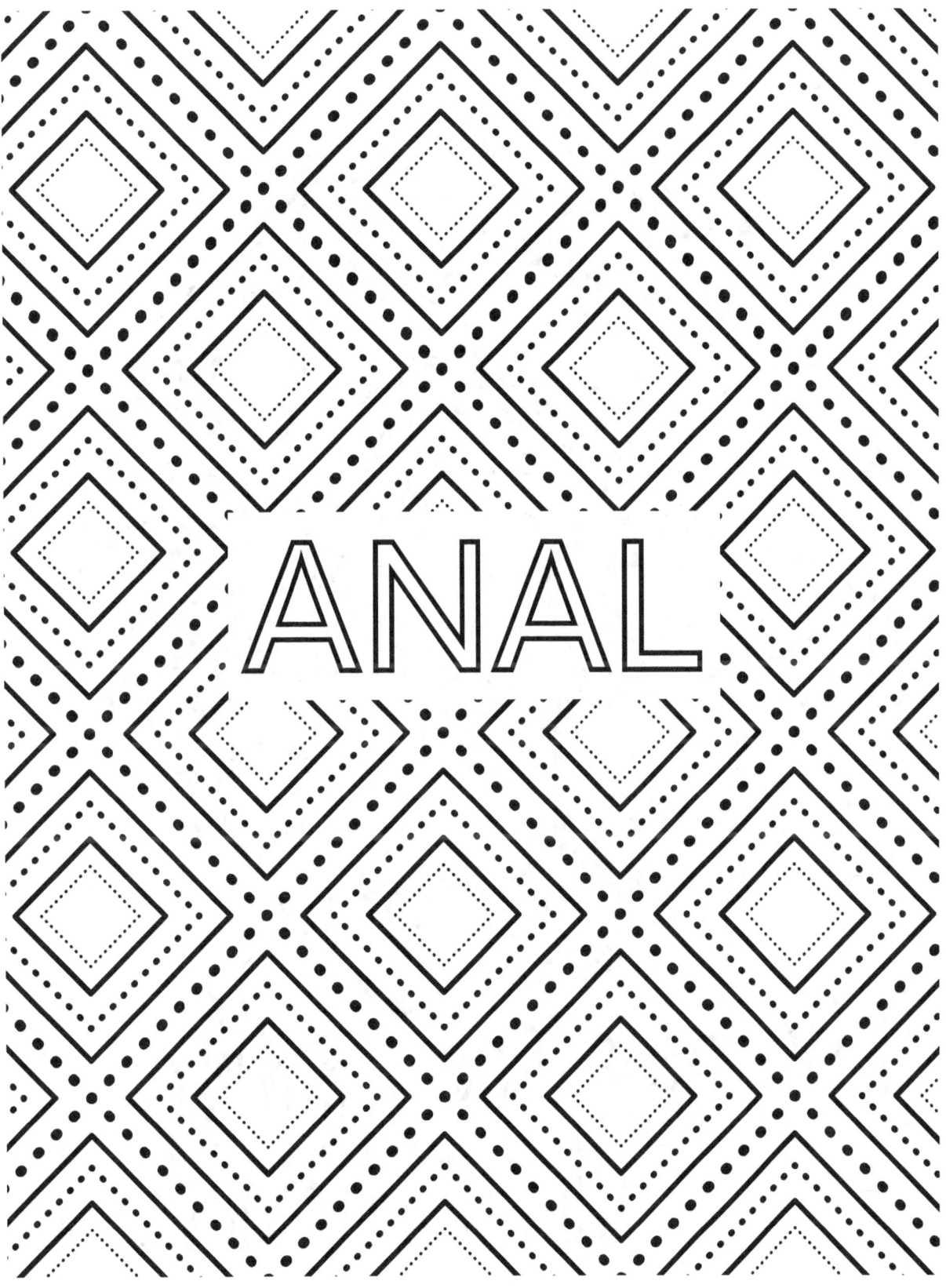

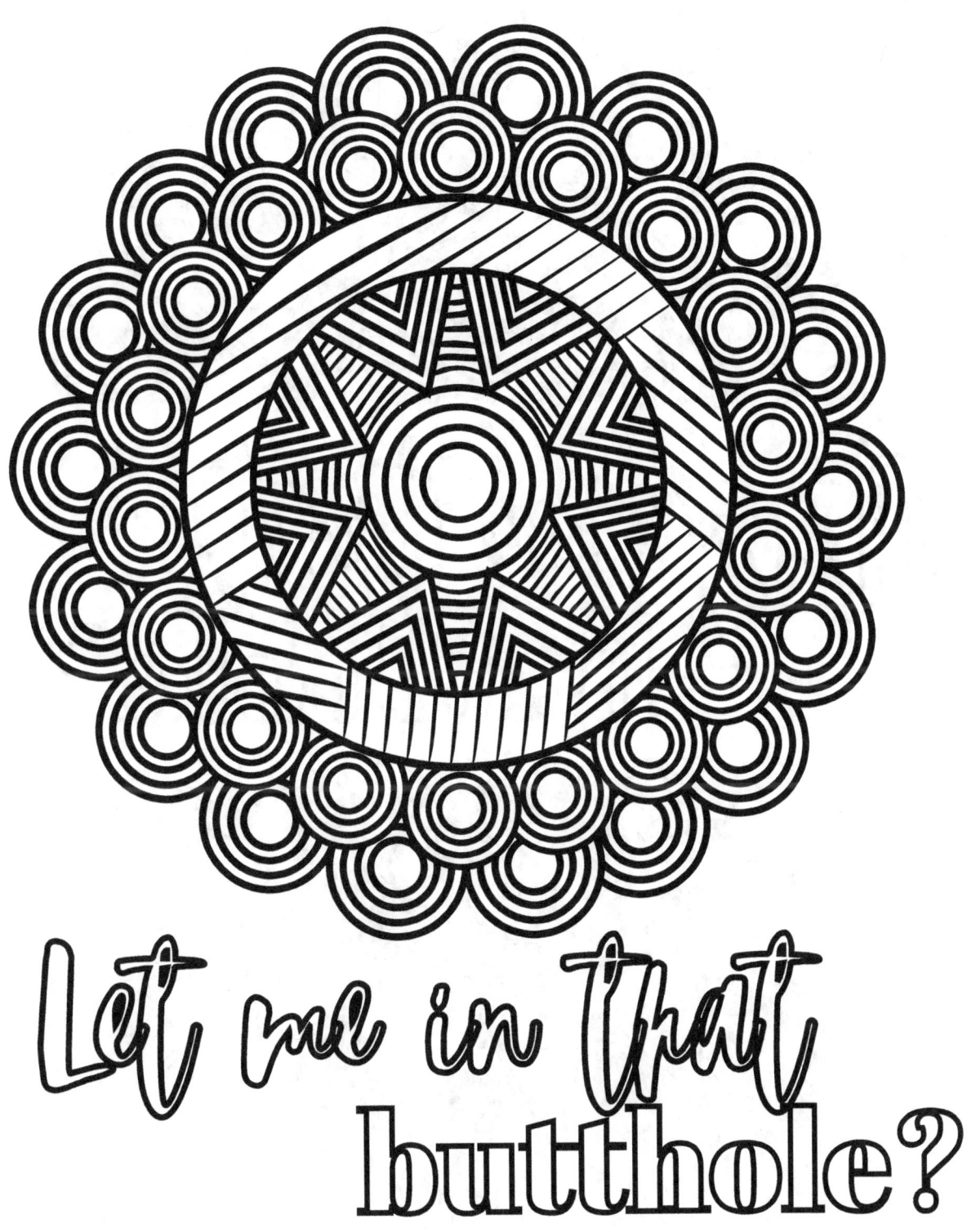

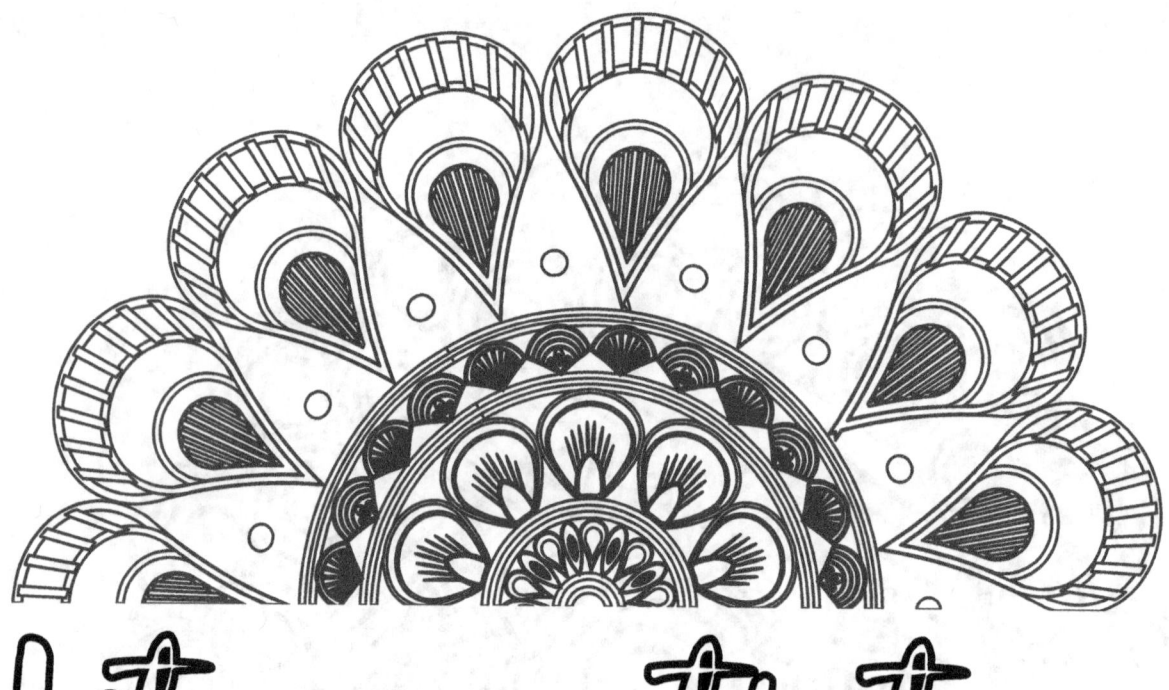

Let me in that butthole?

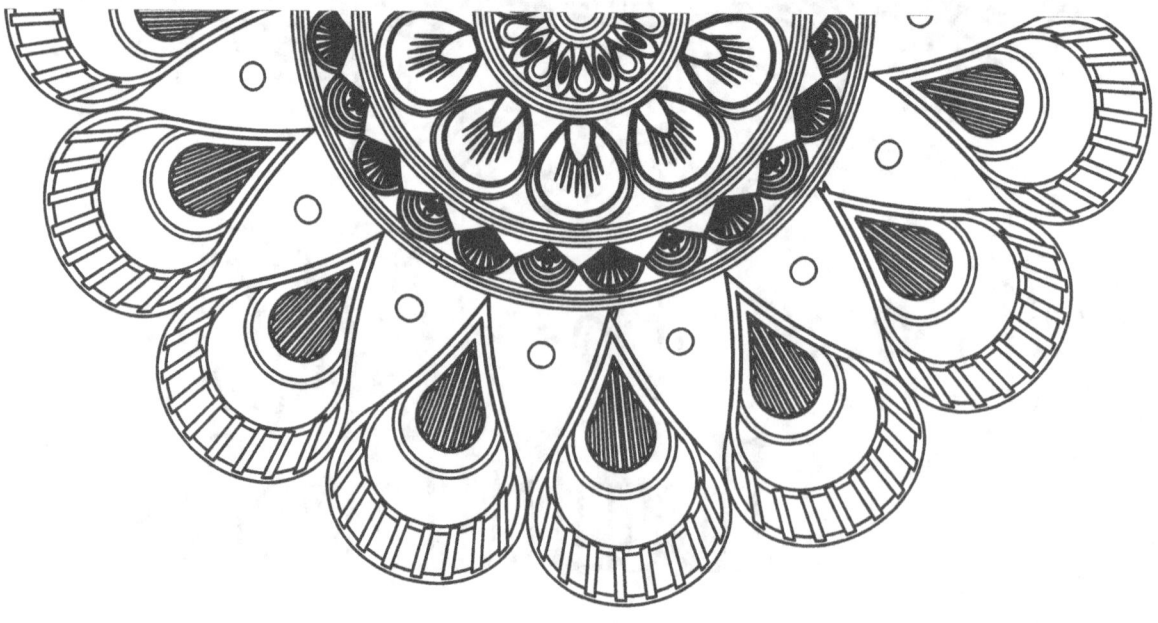

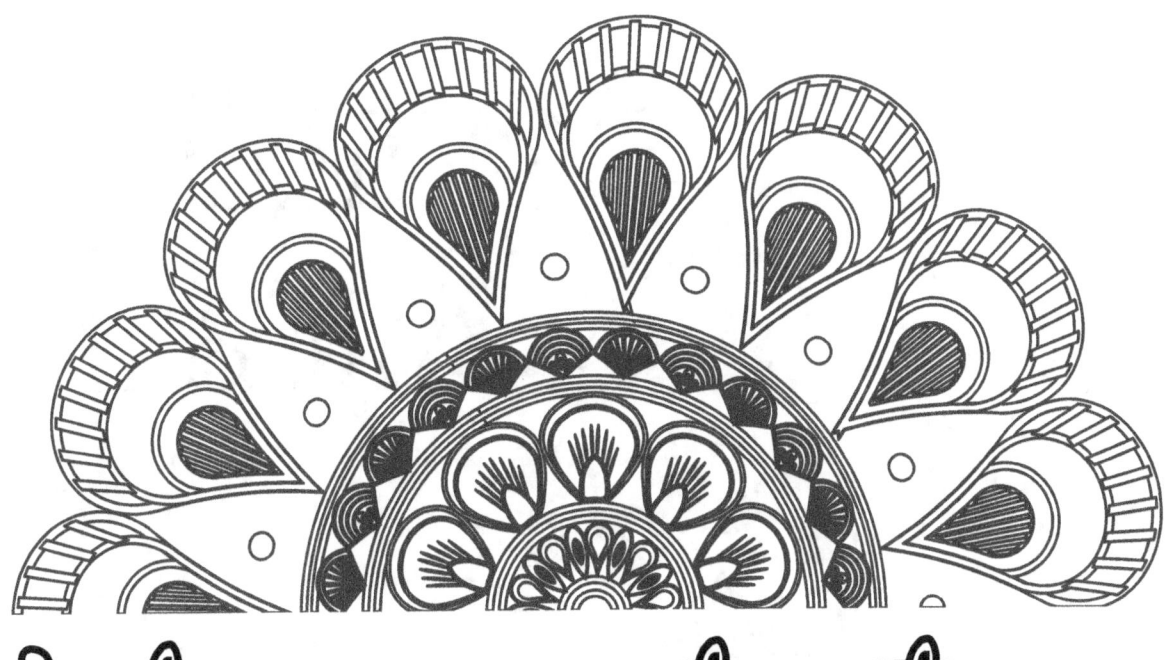

Let me in that butthole?

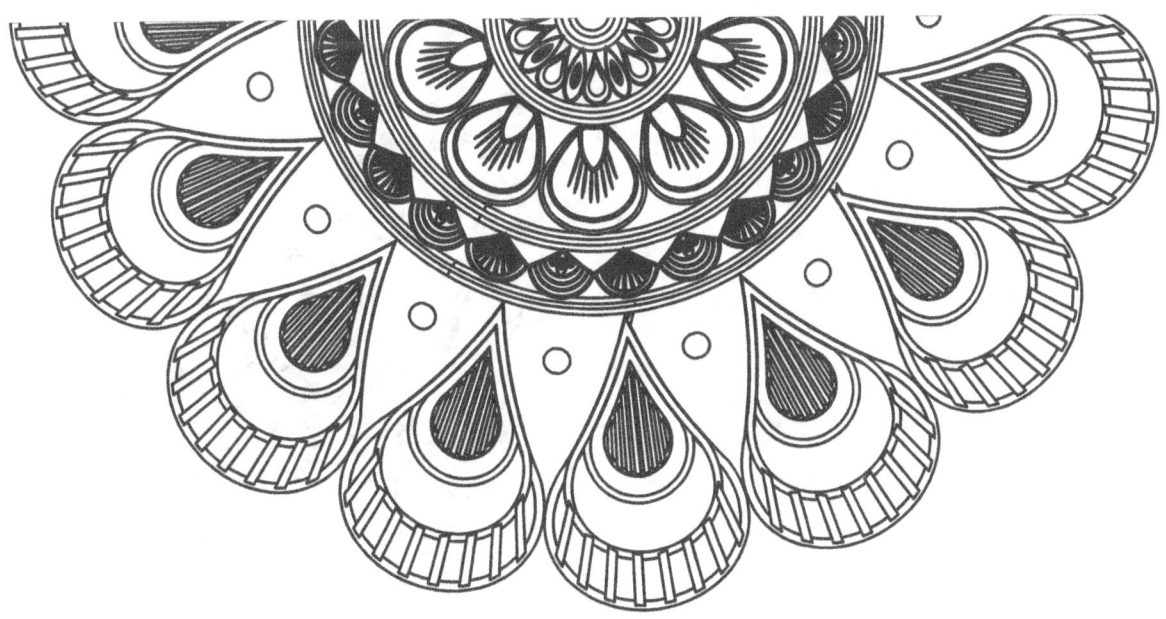

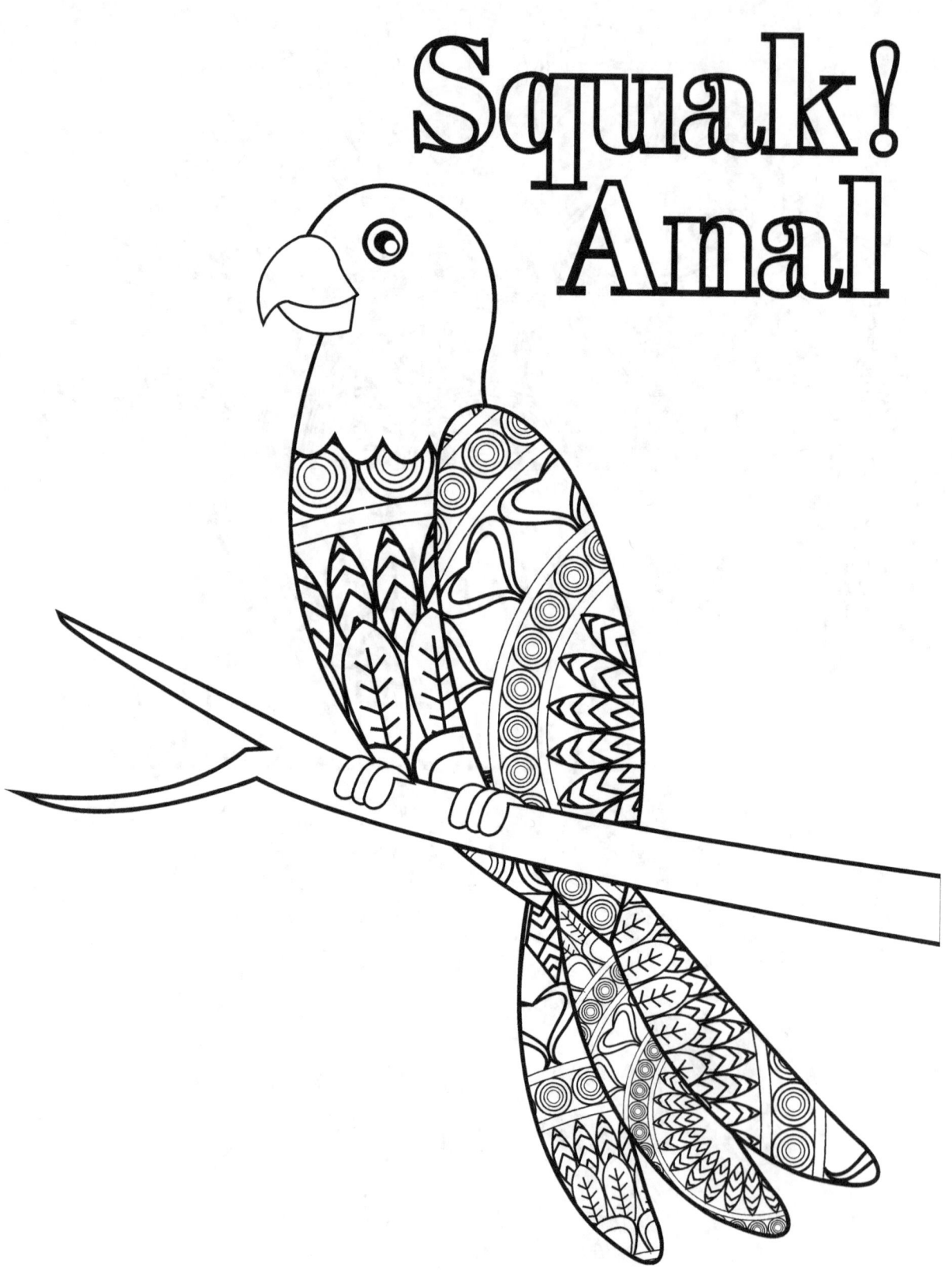

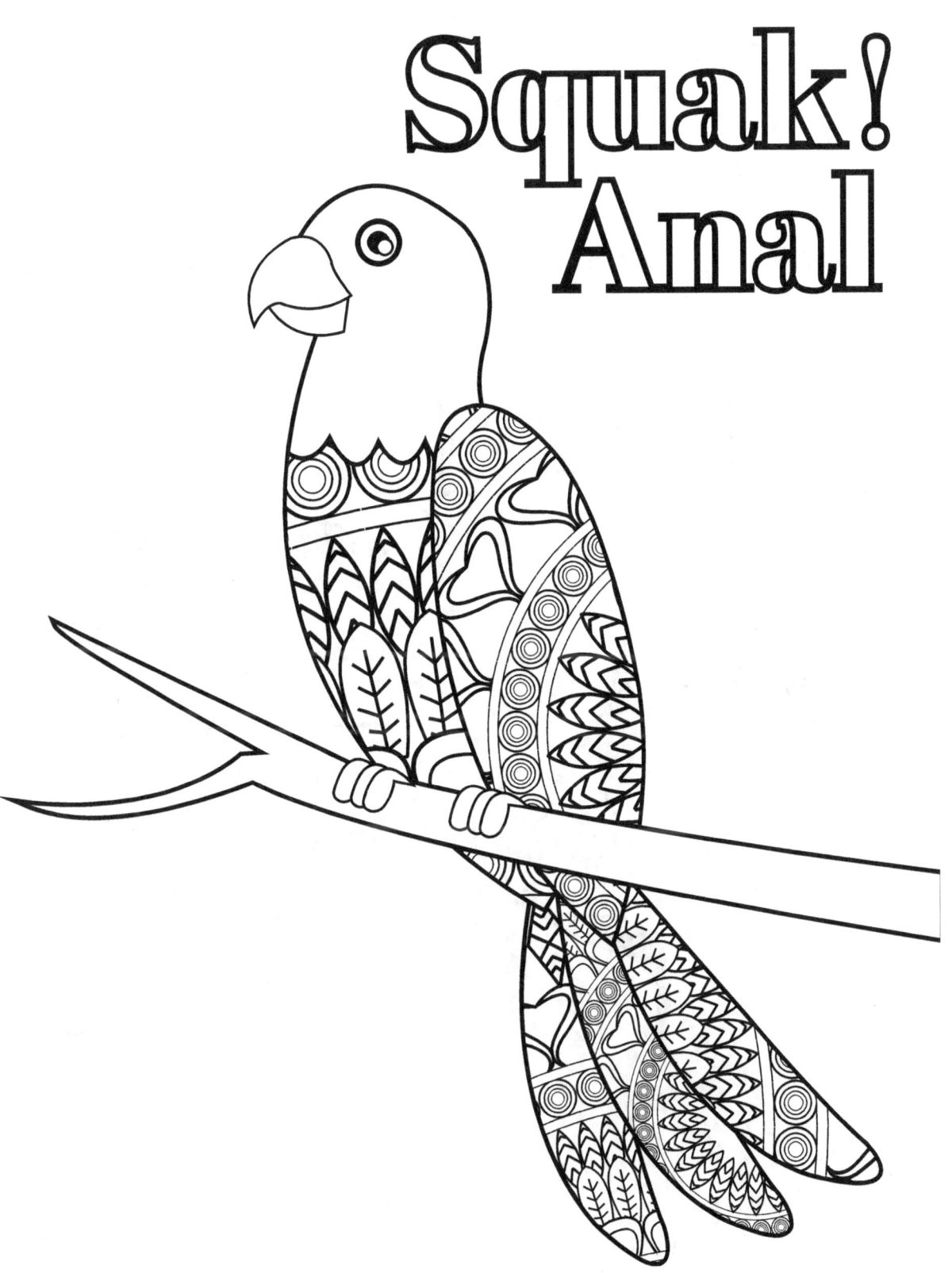

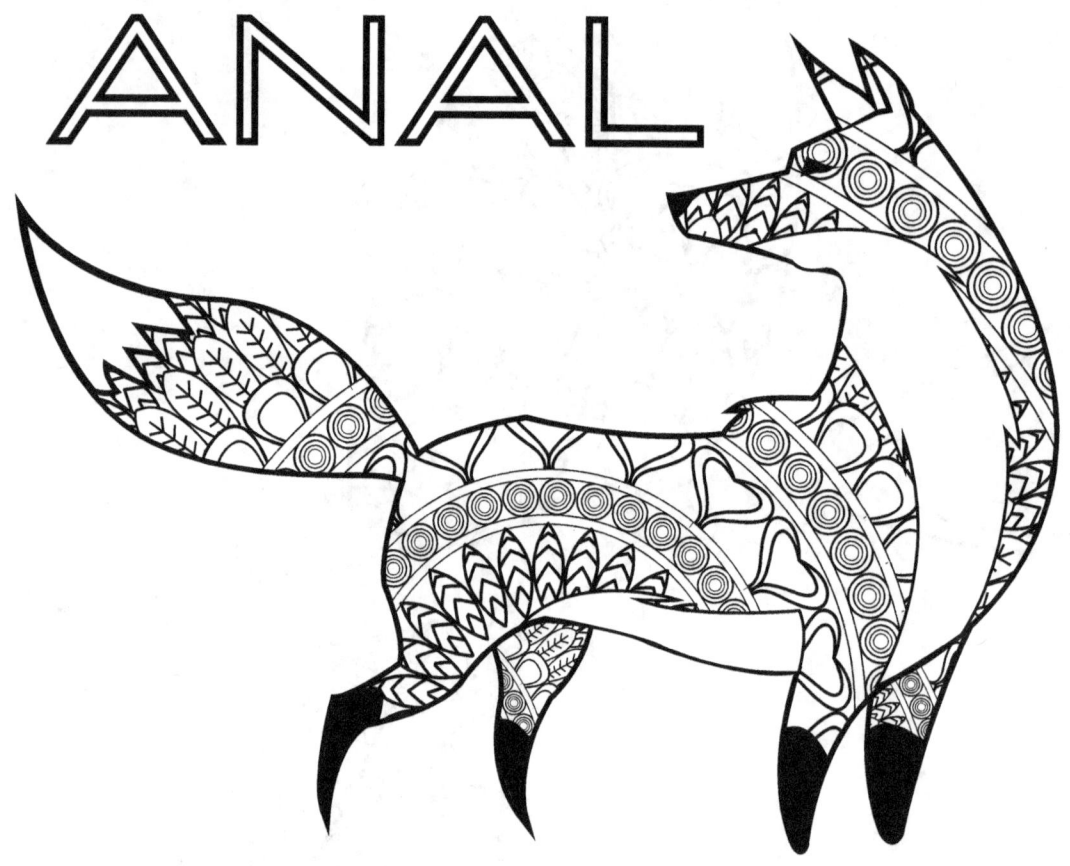

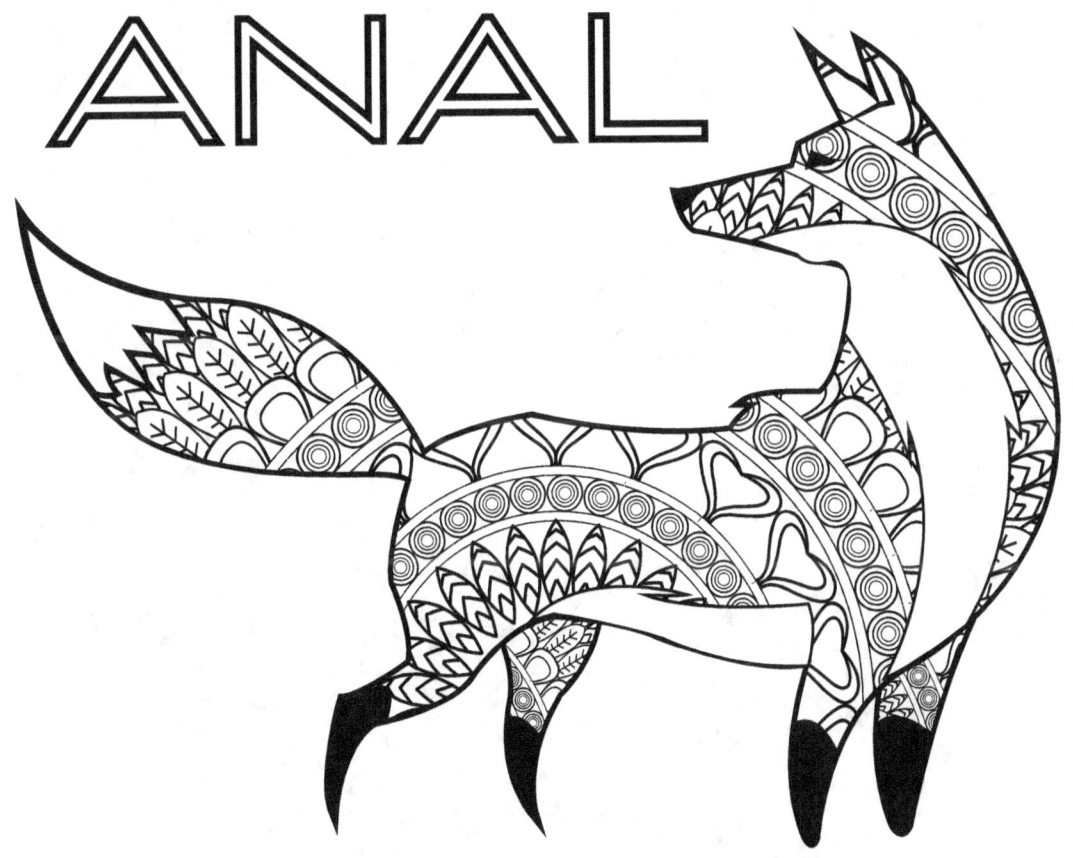

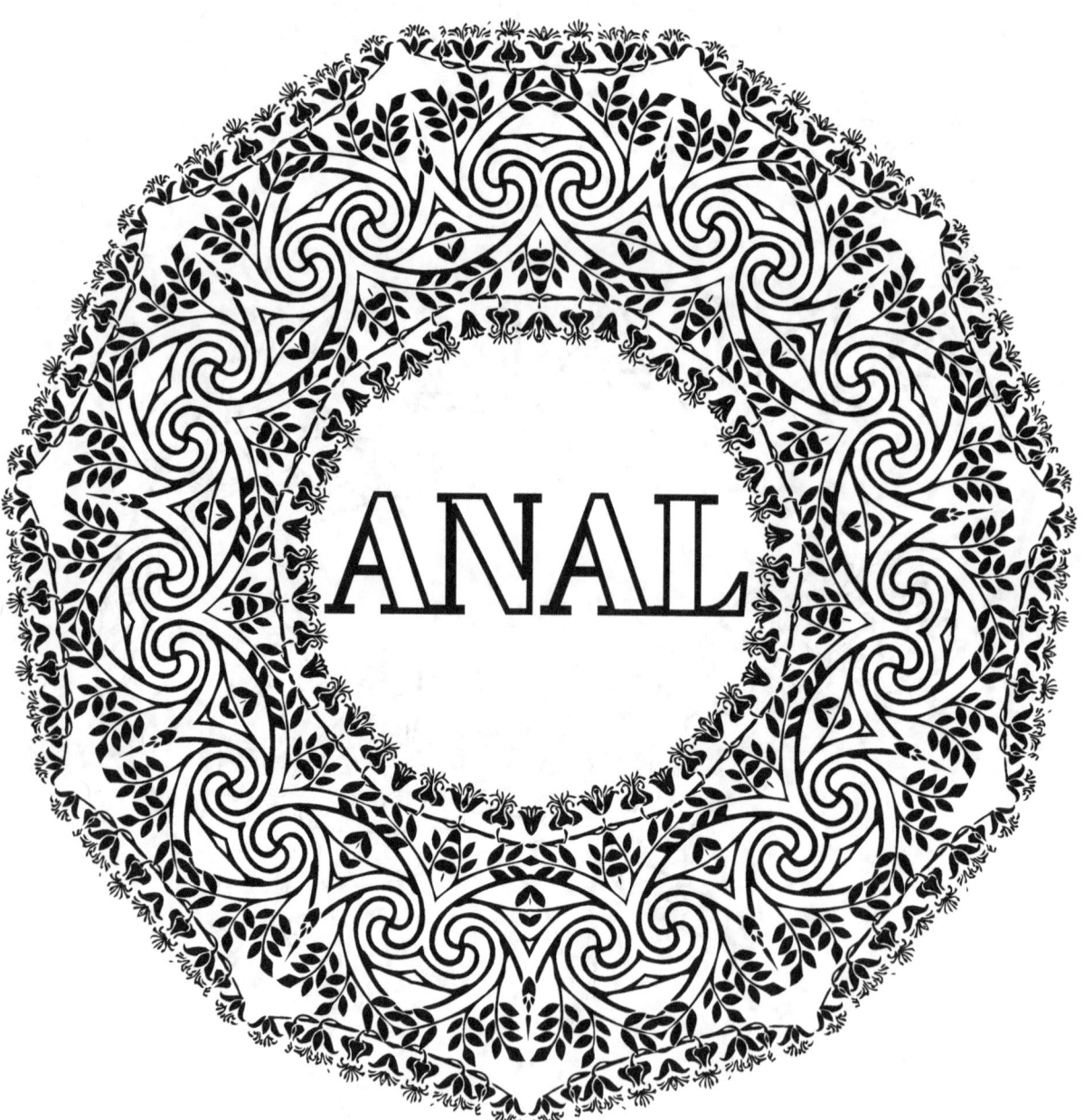

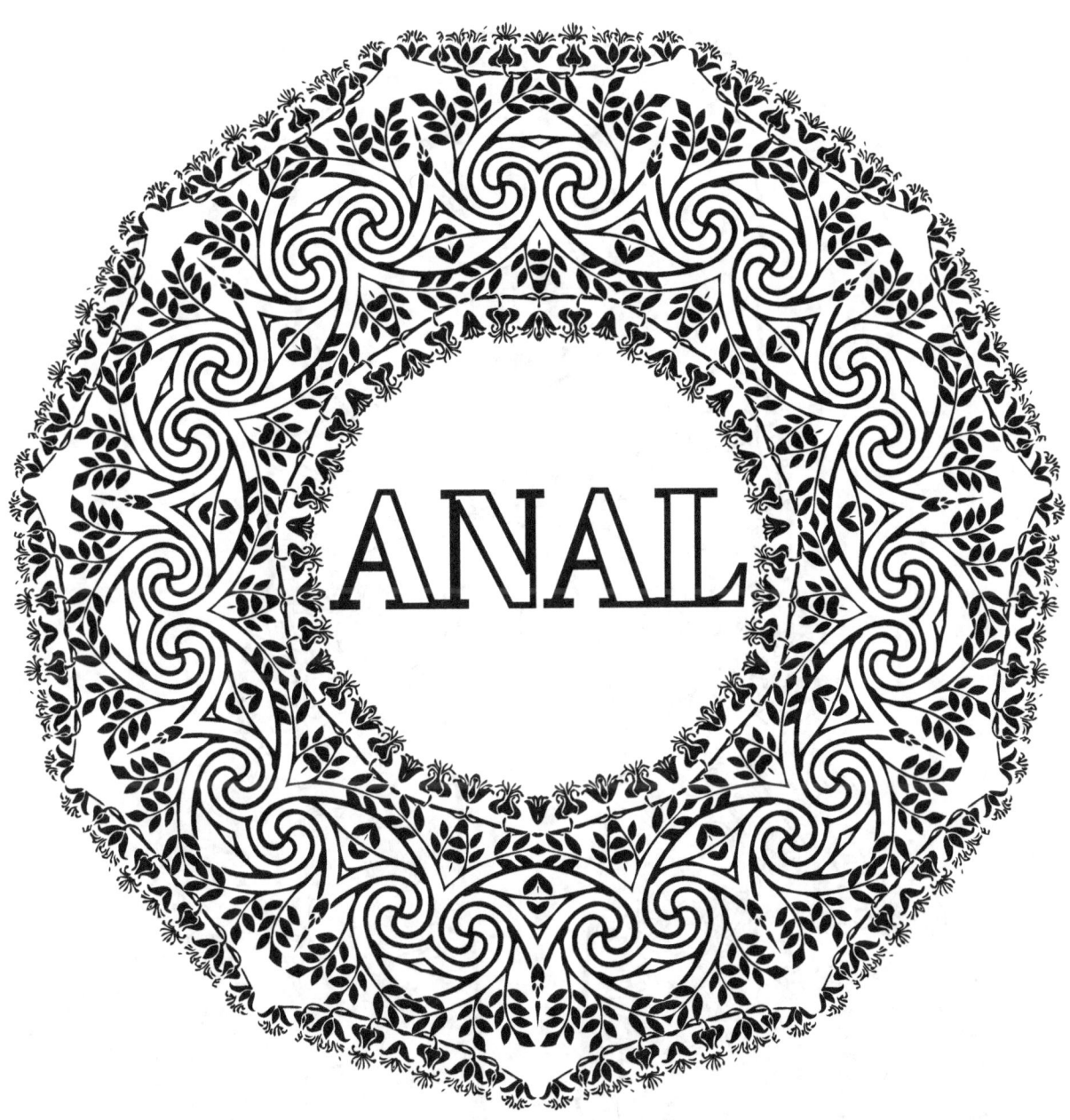

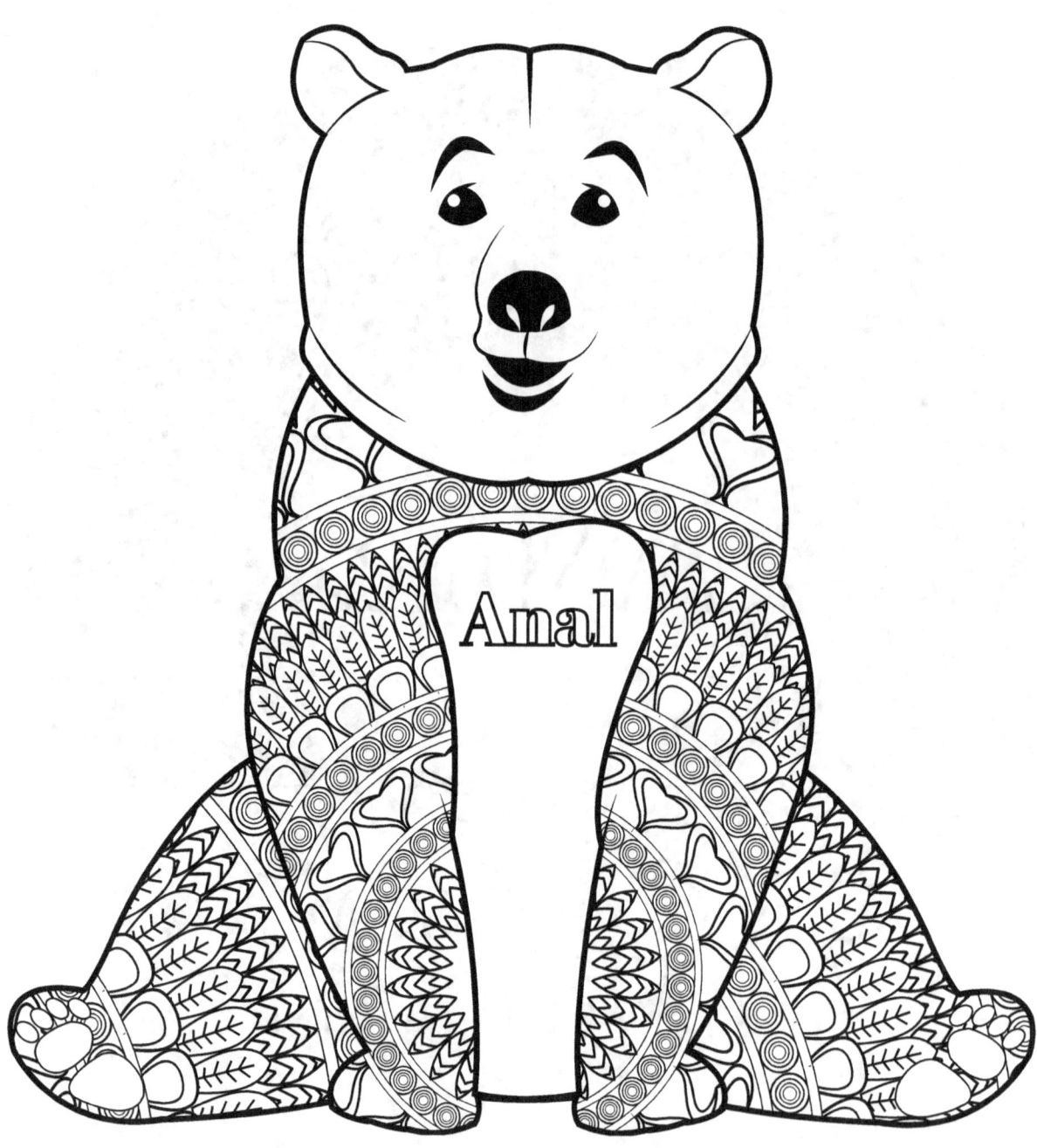

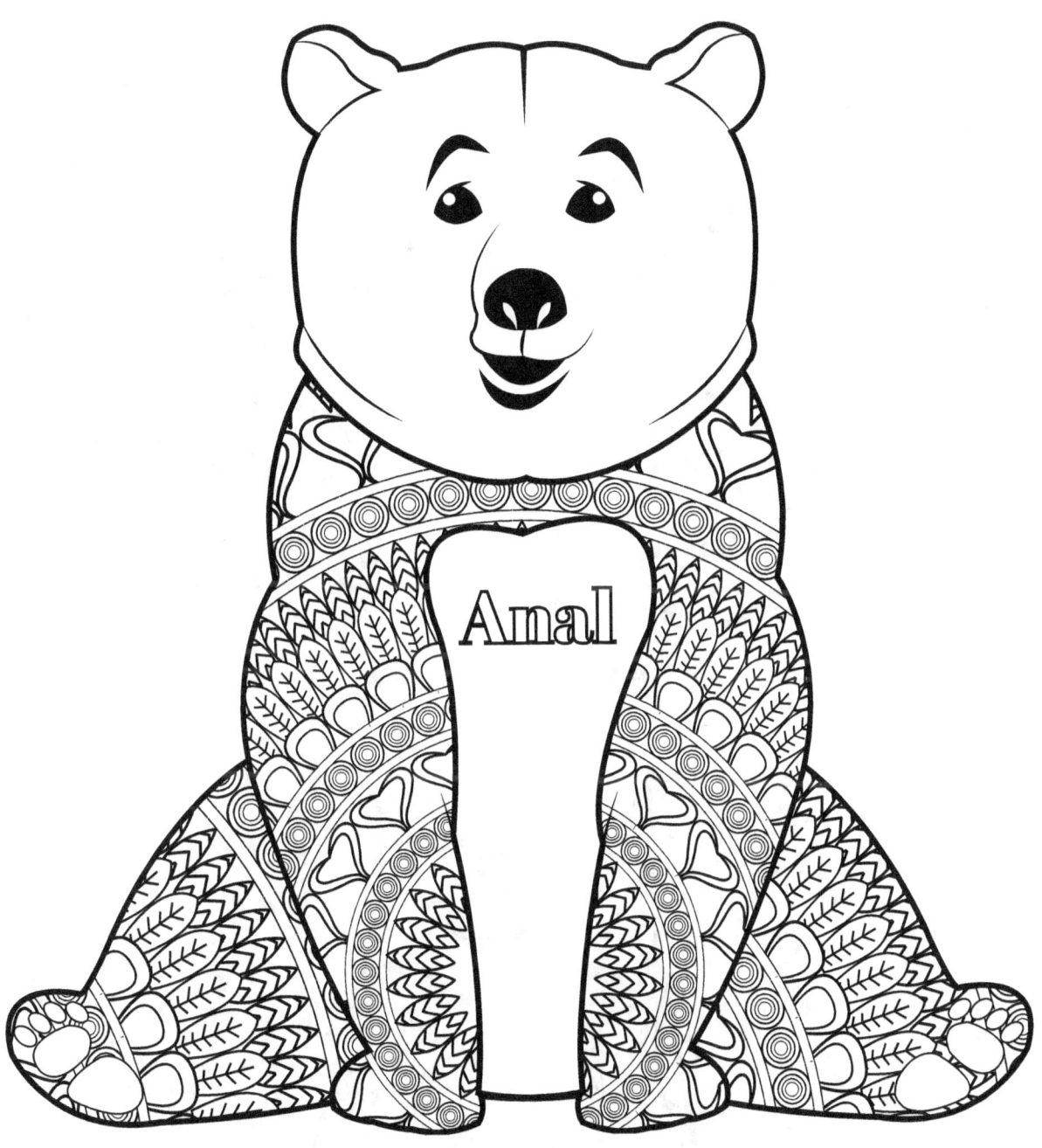

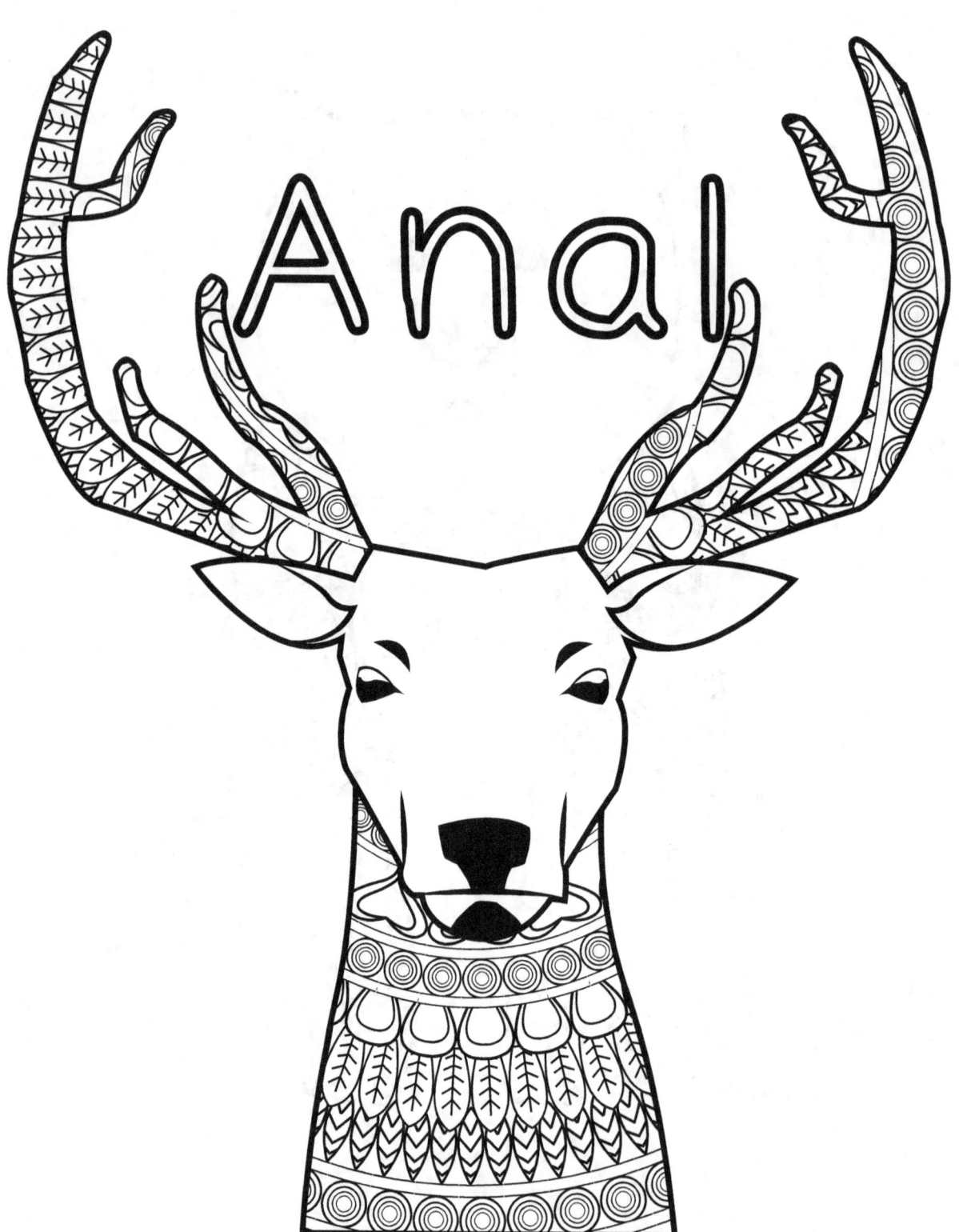

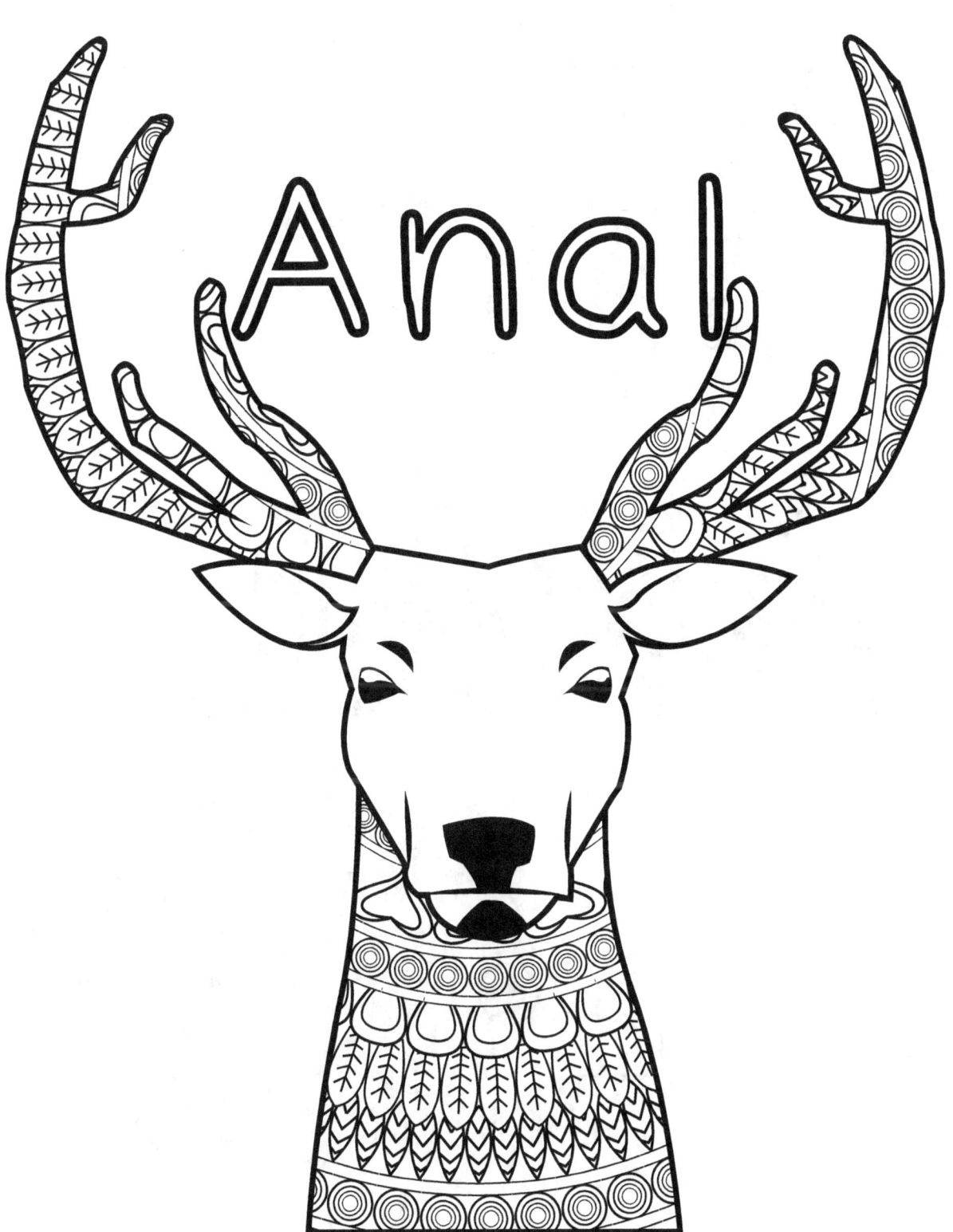

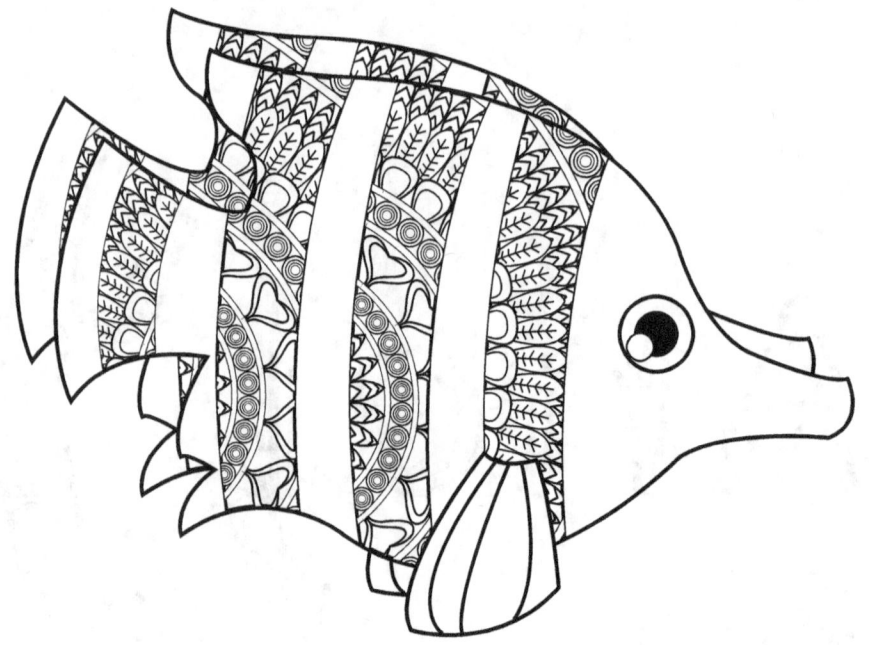

ANAL

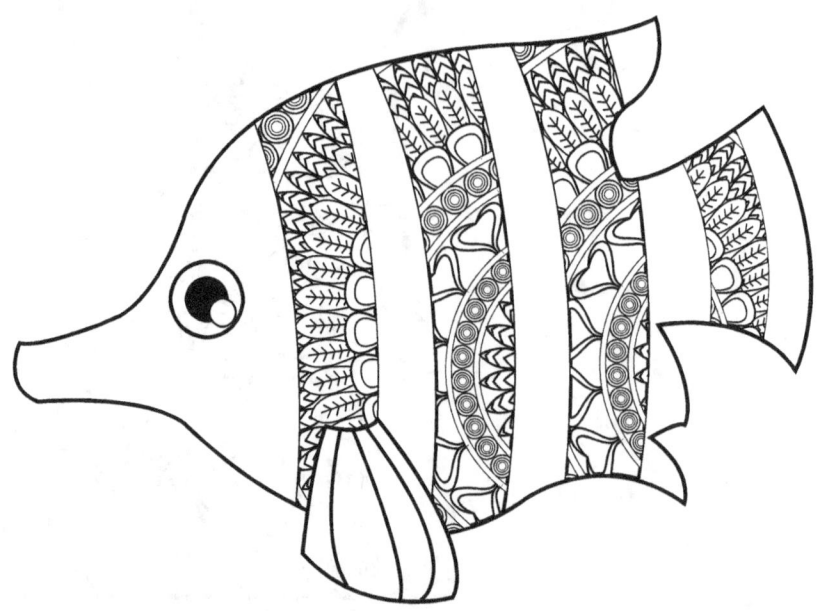

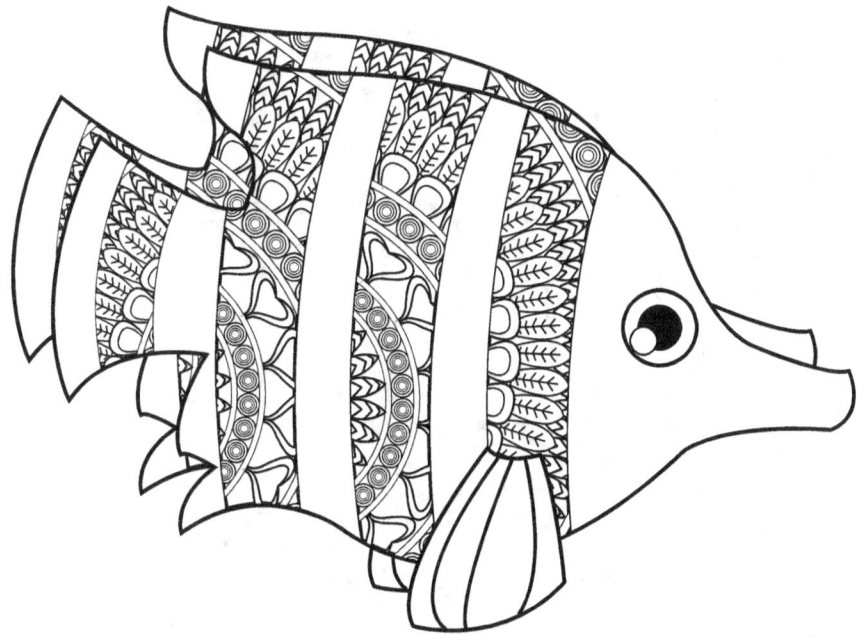

ANAL

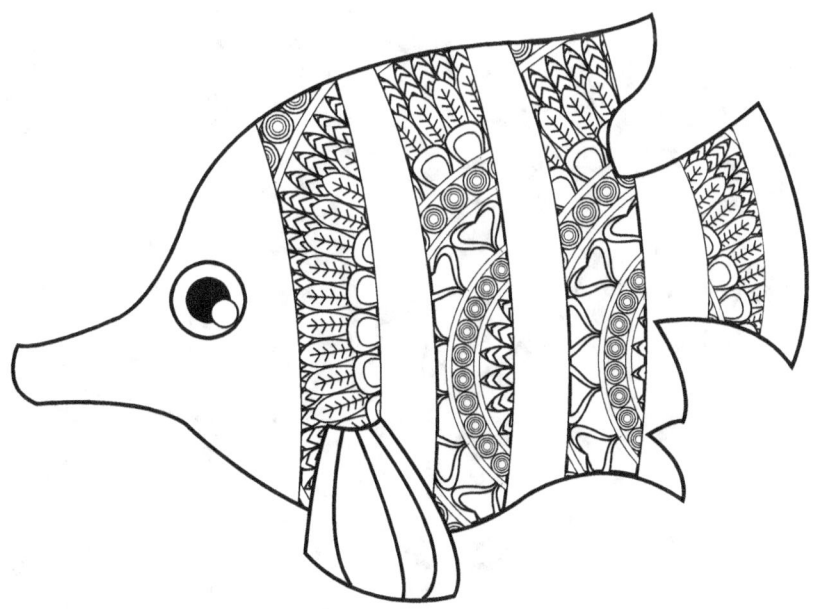

BOOTY WORK

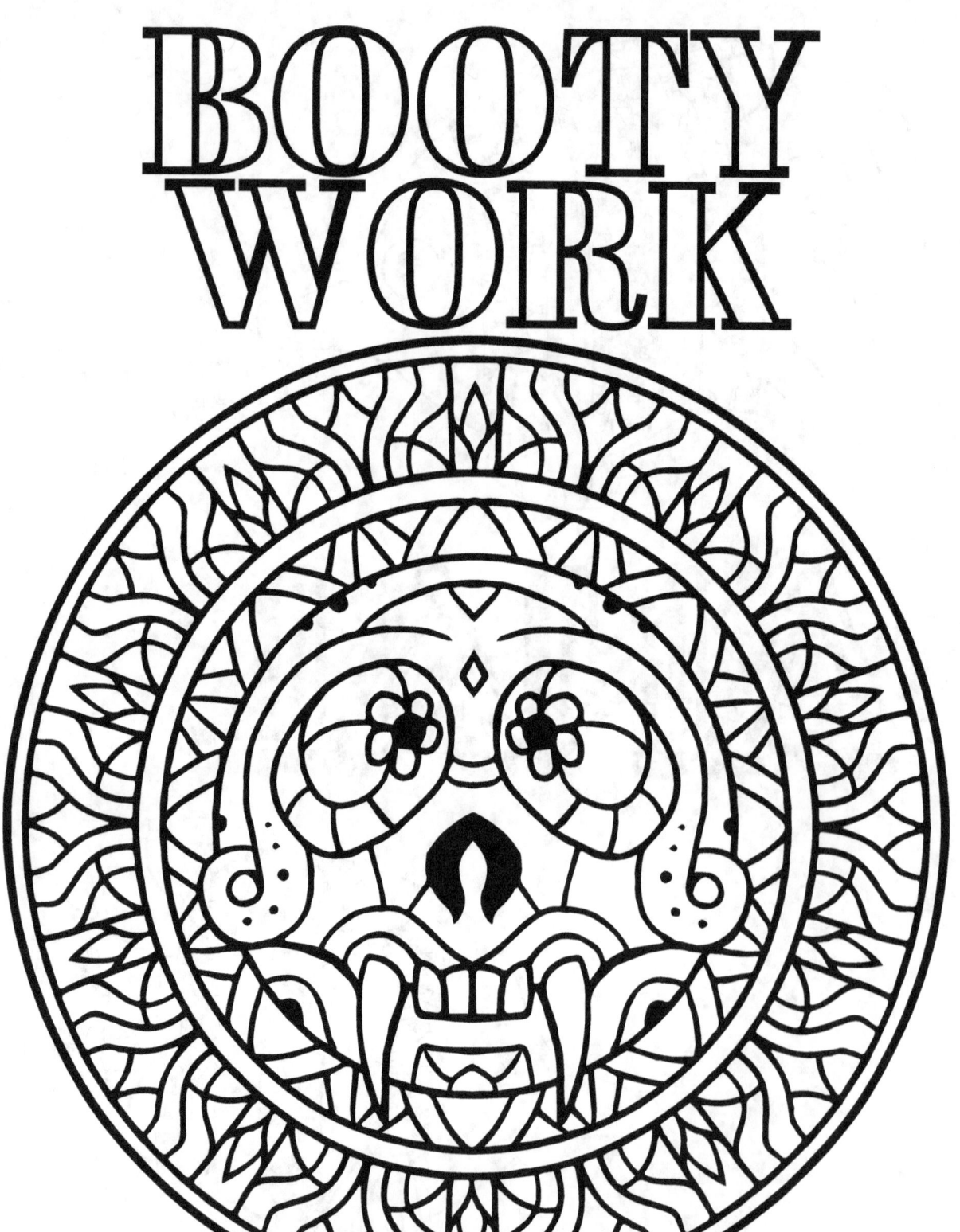

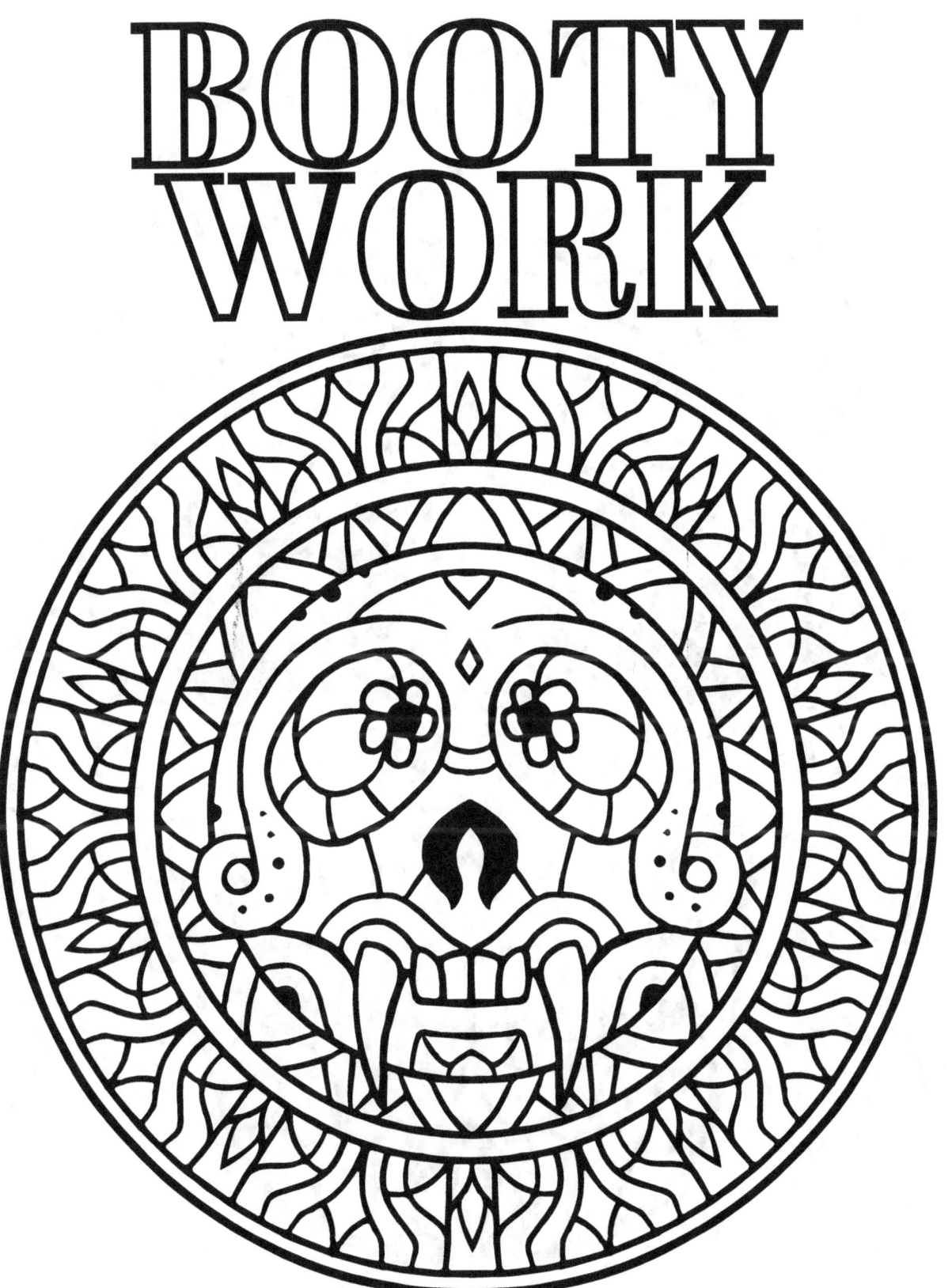

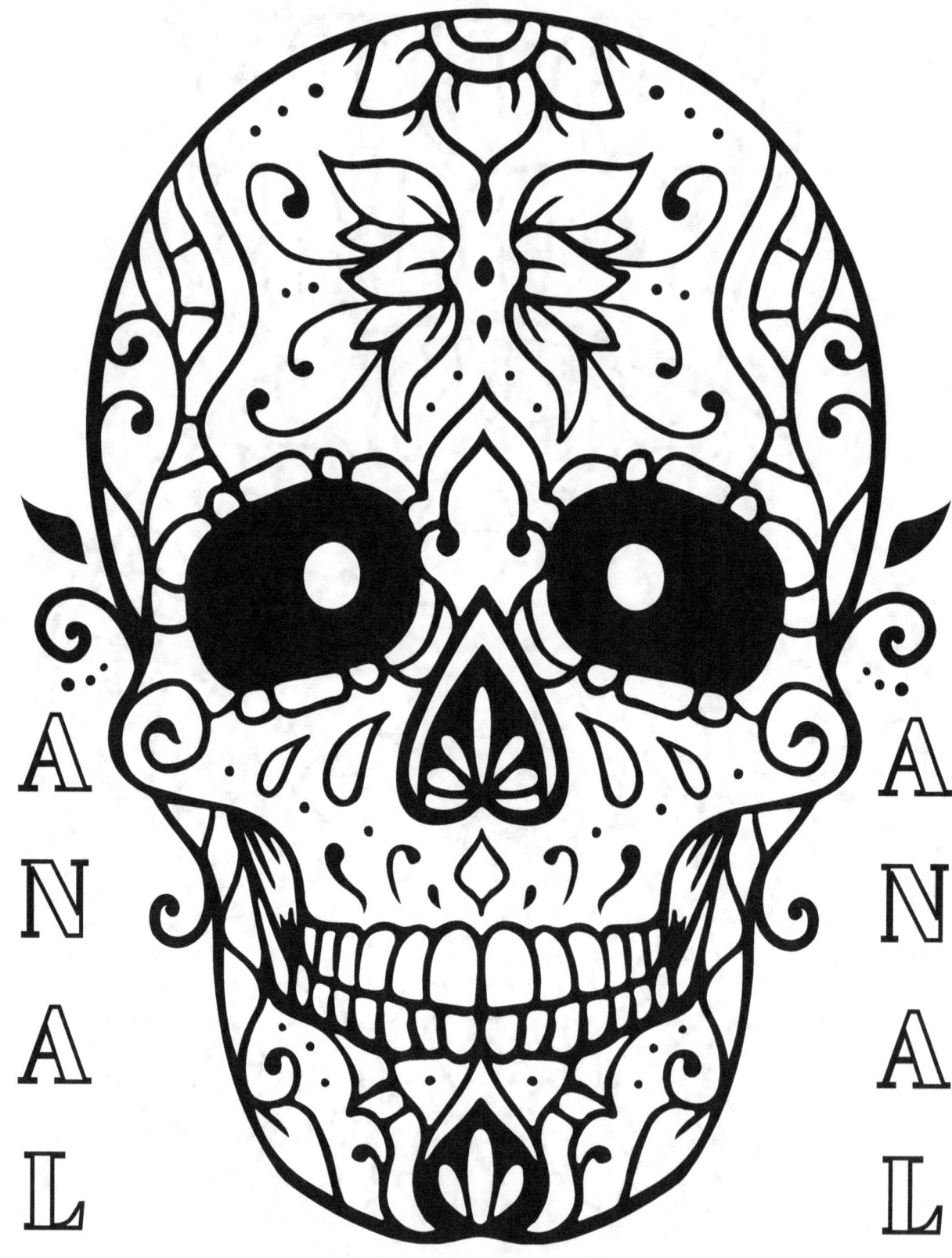

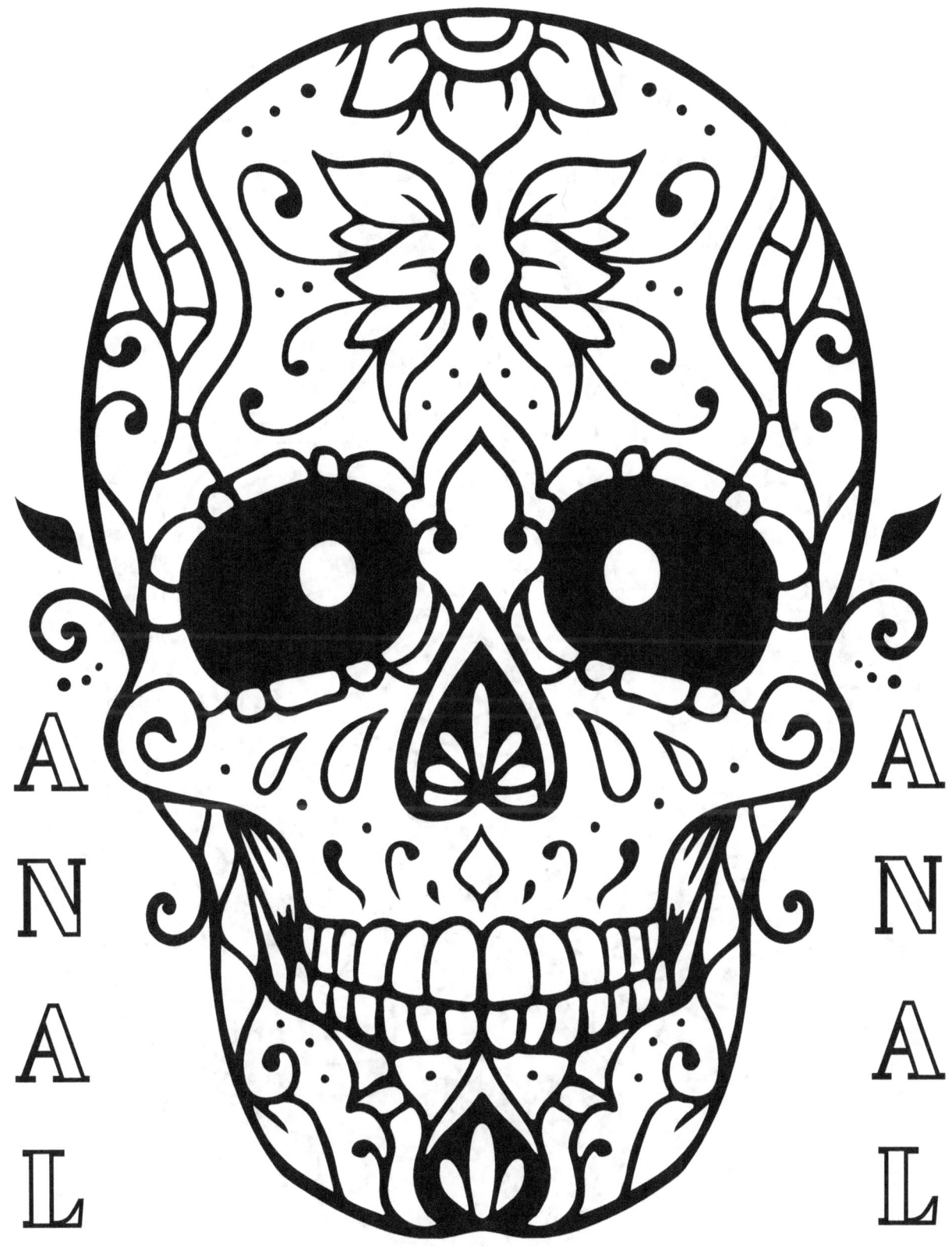

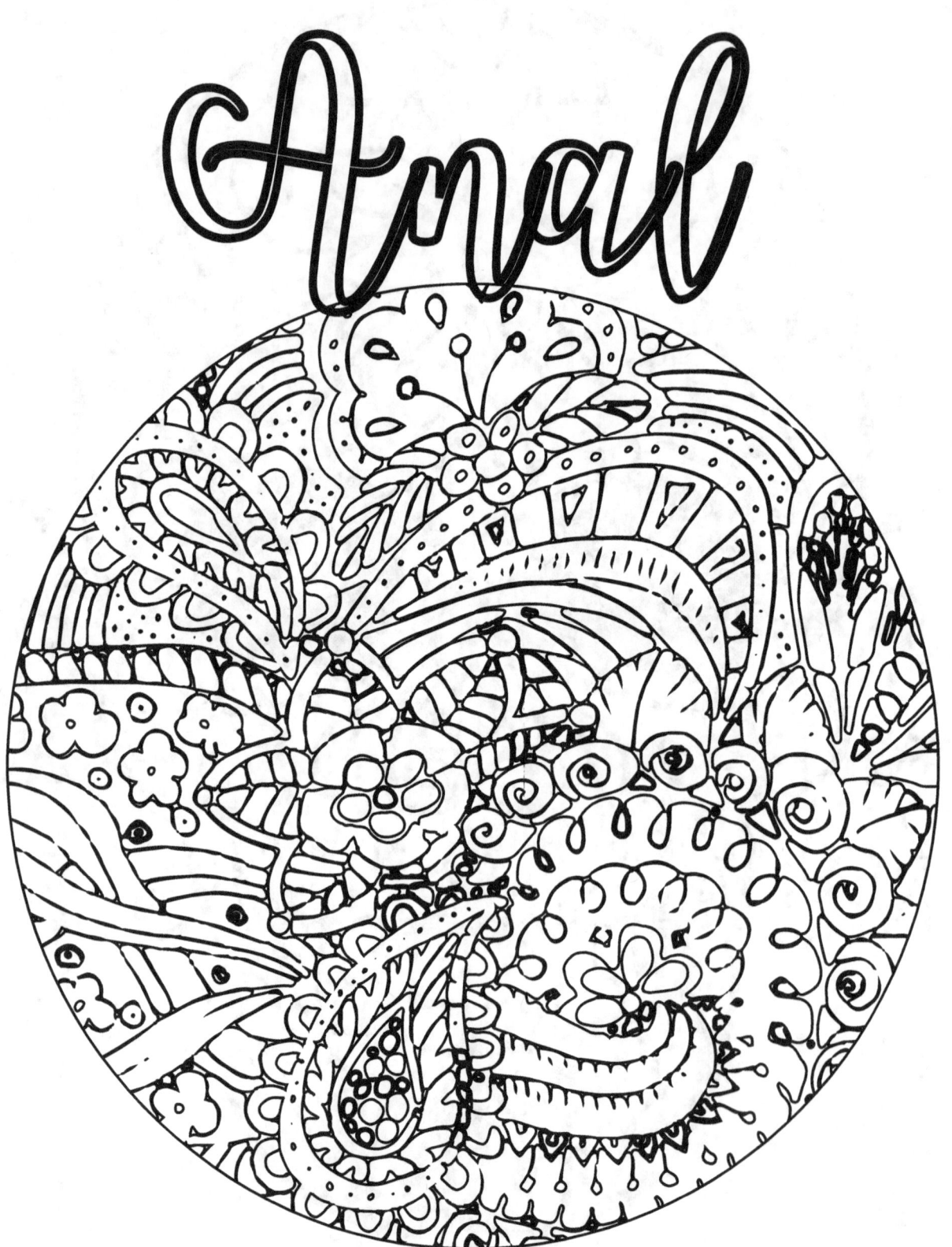

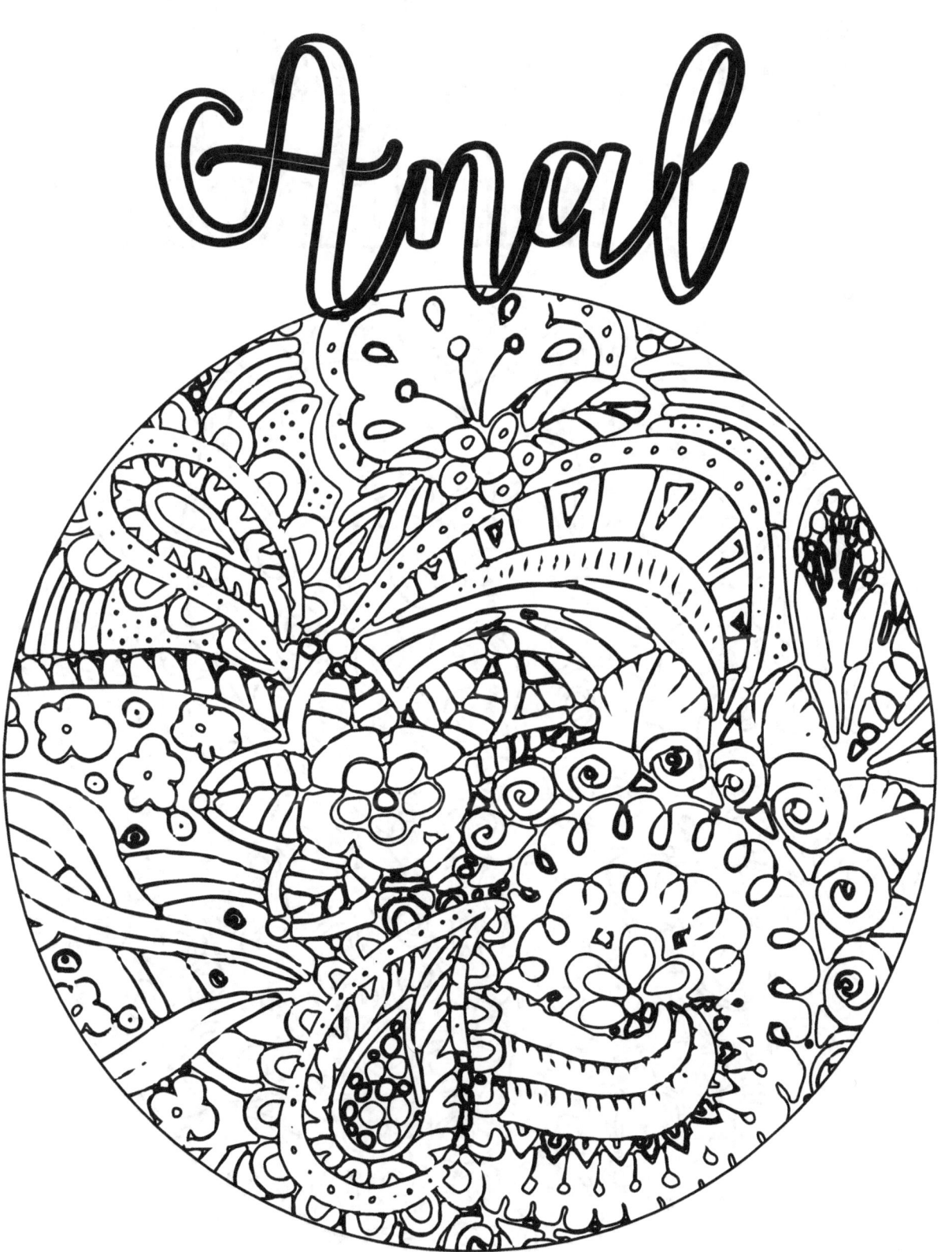

Let me in that butthole?

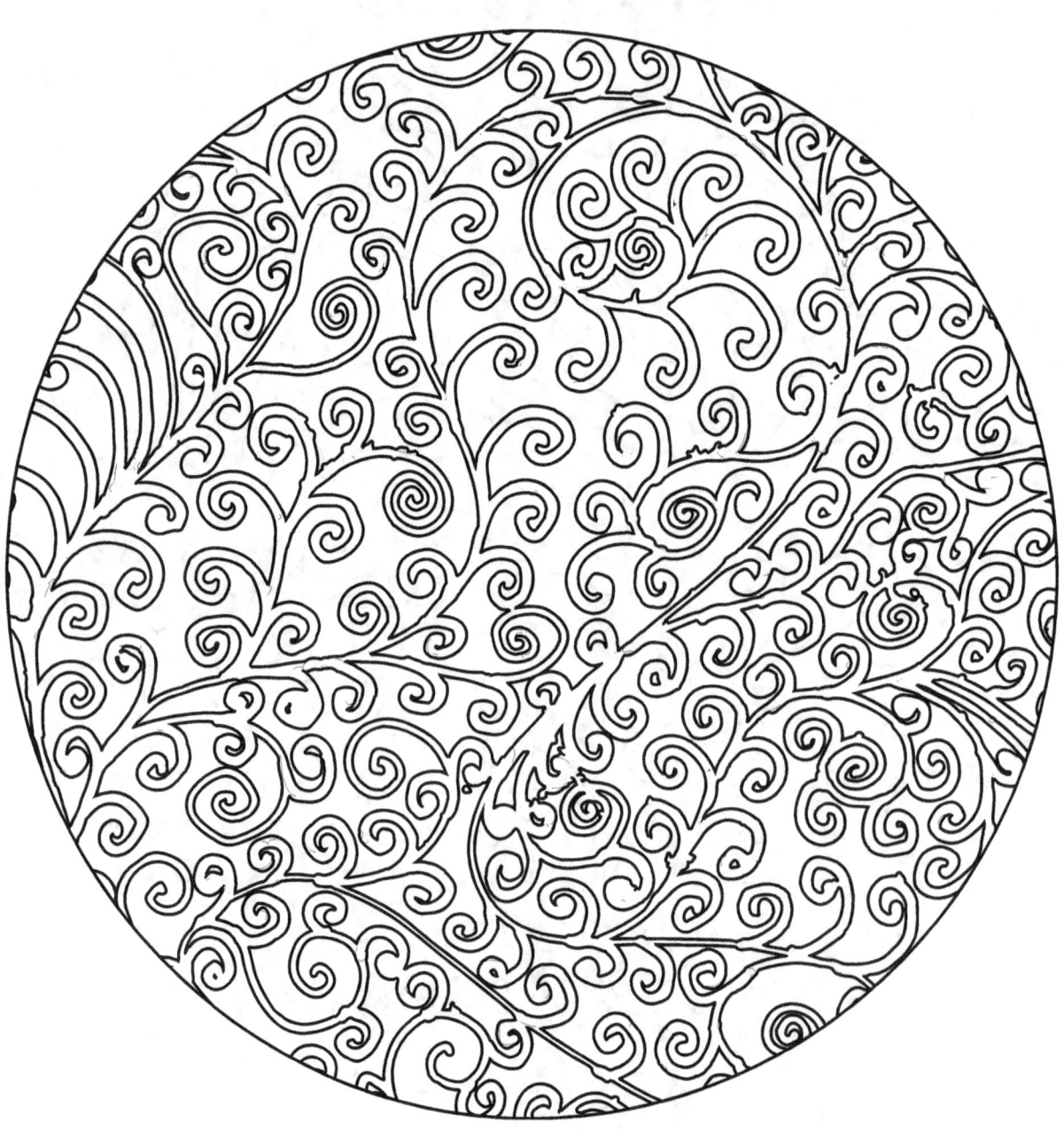

Let me in that butthole?

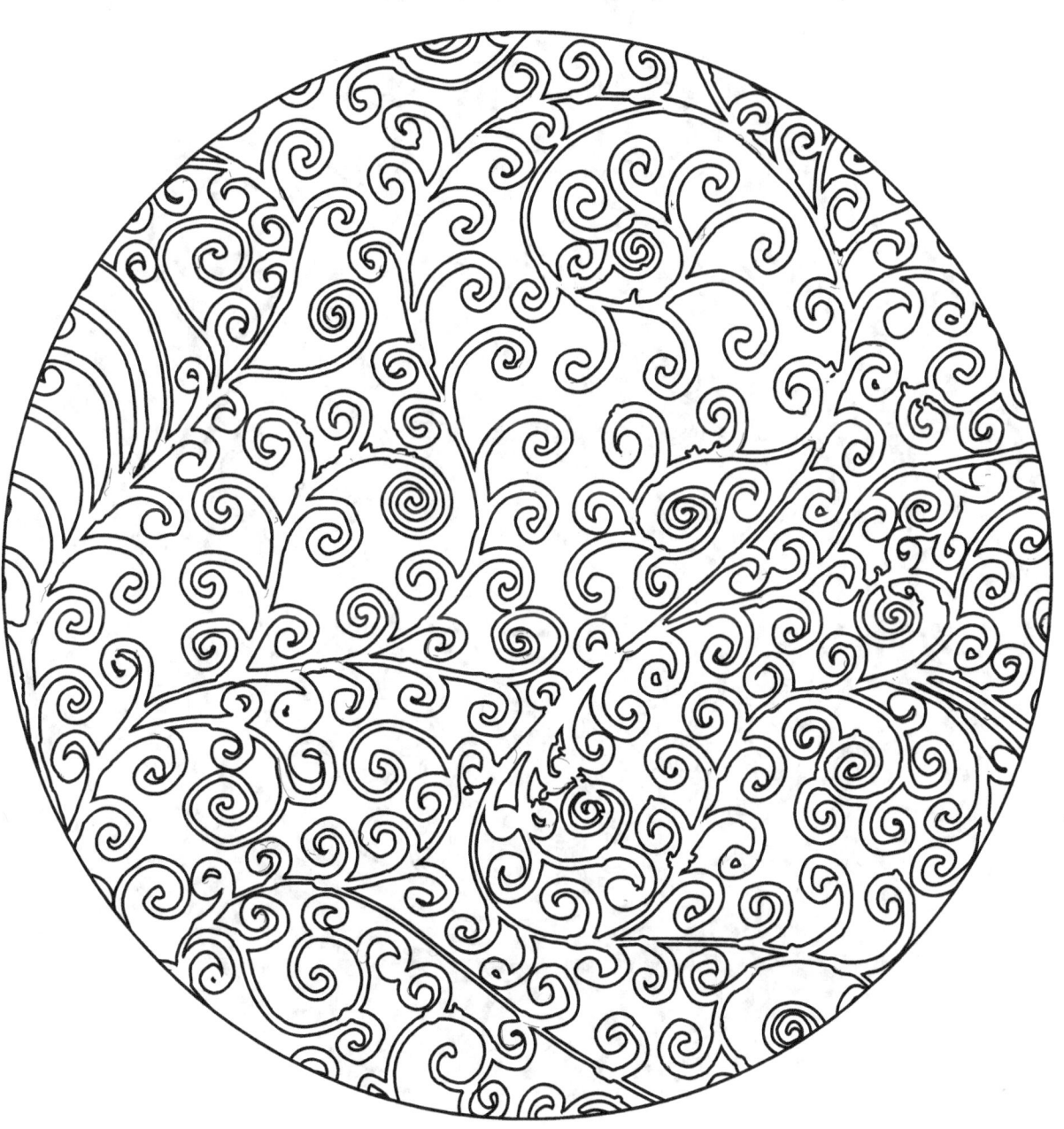

anal?

anal?

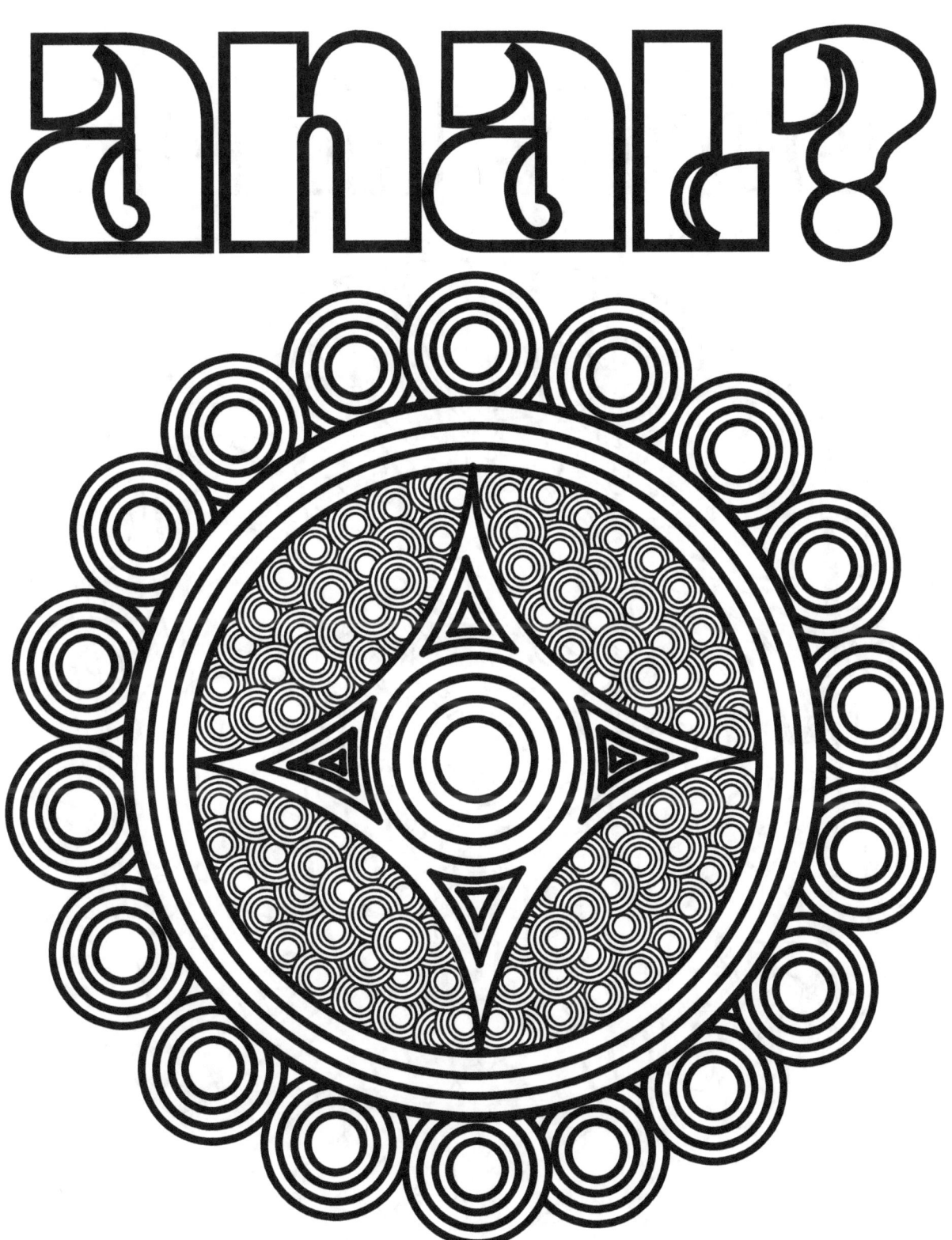

booty time!

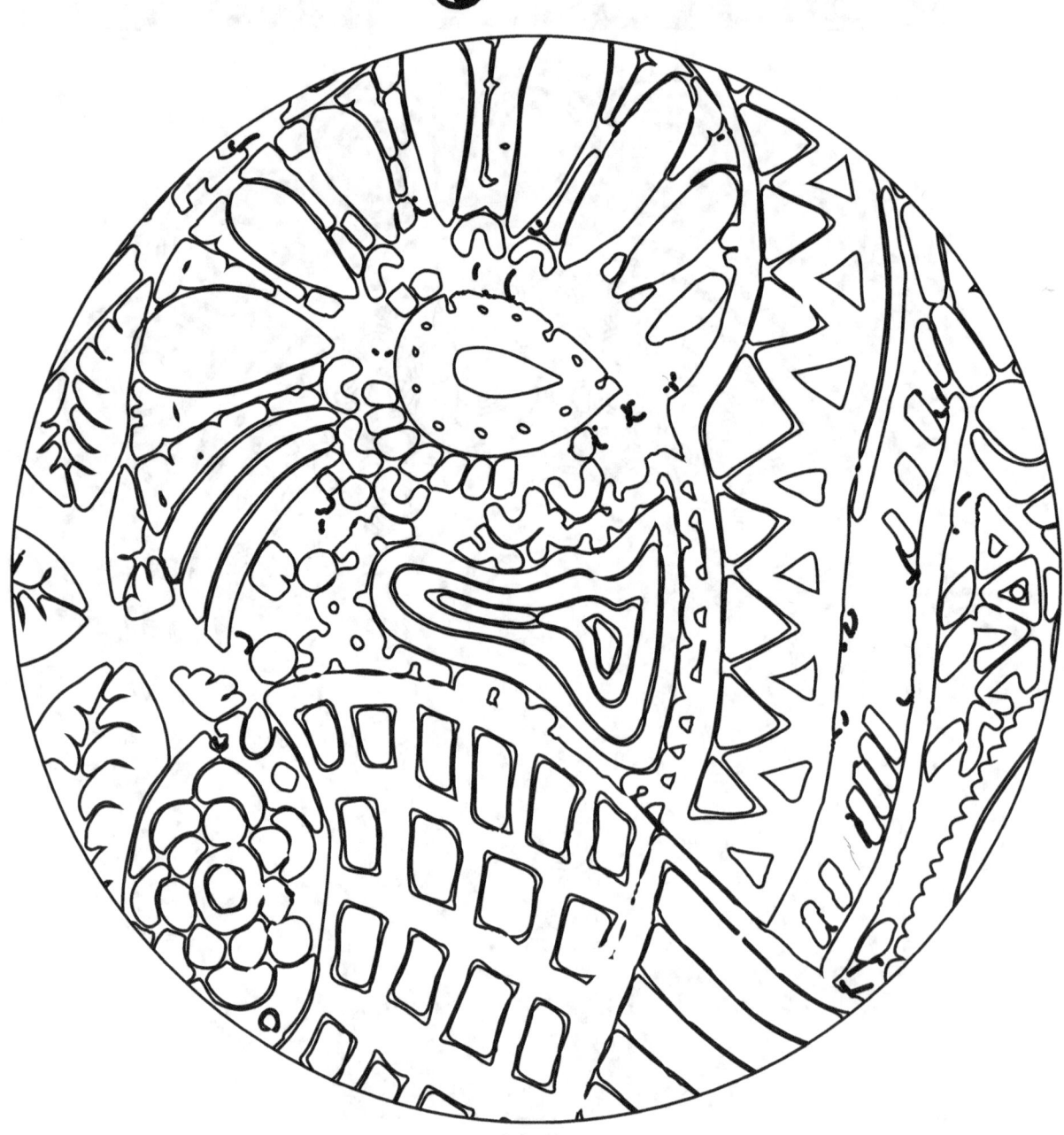

booty time!

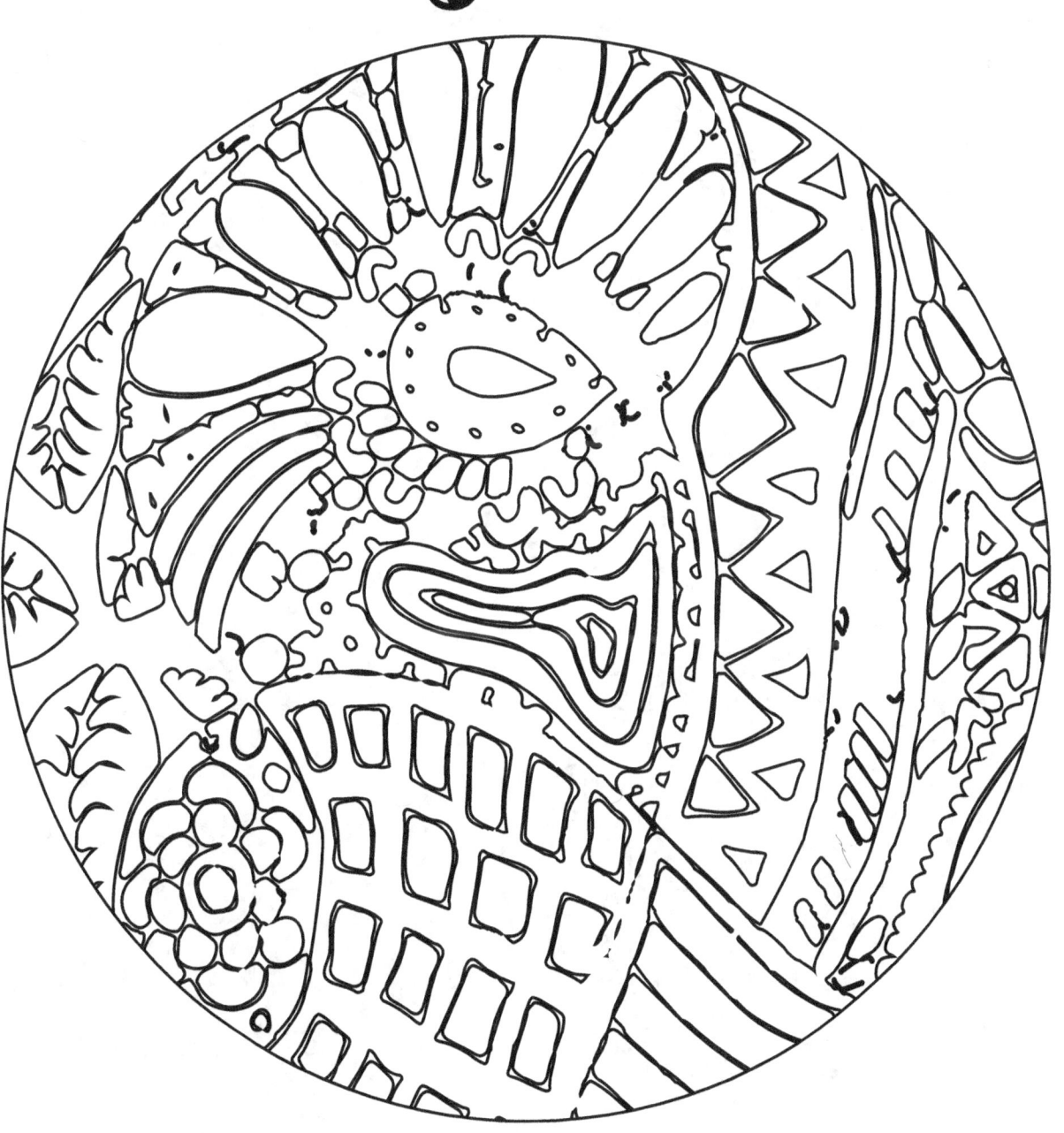

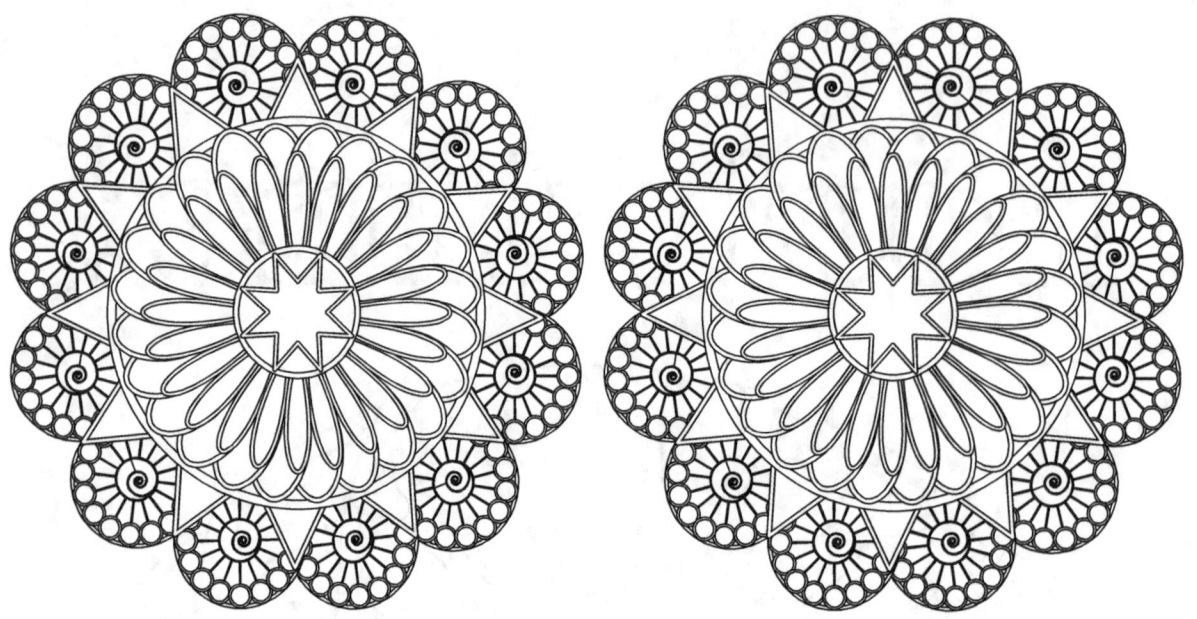

You. Me. In the butt.

ANAL

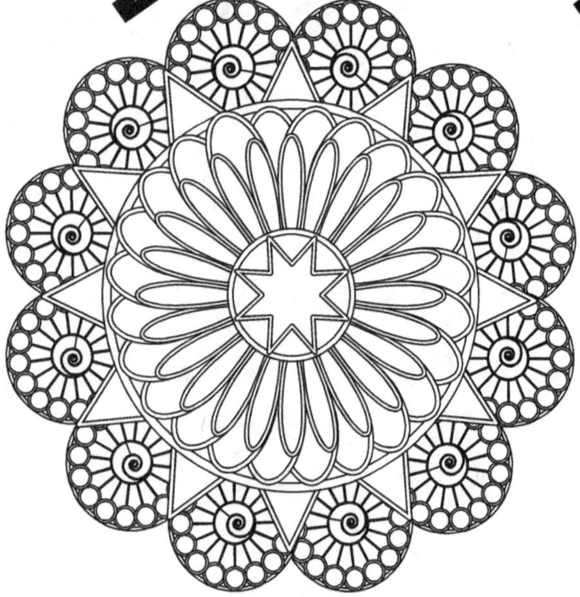

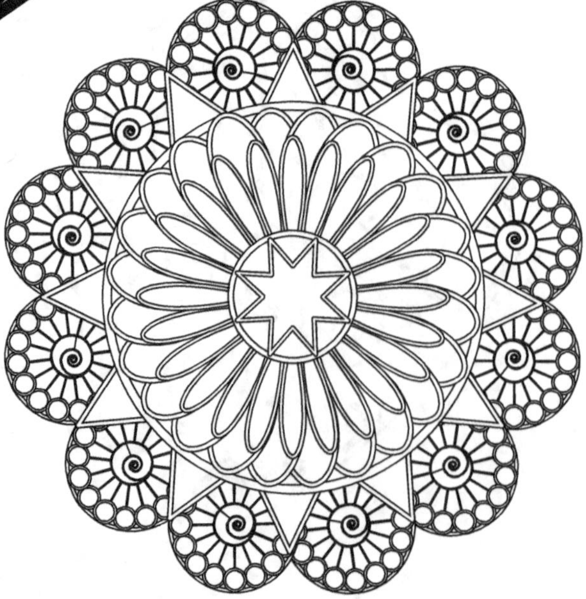

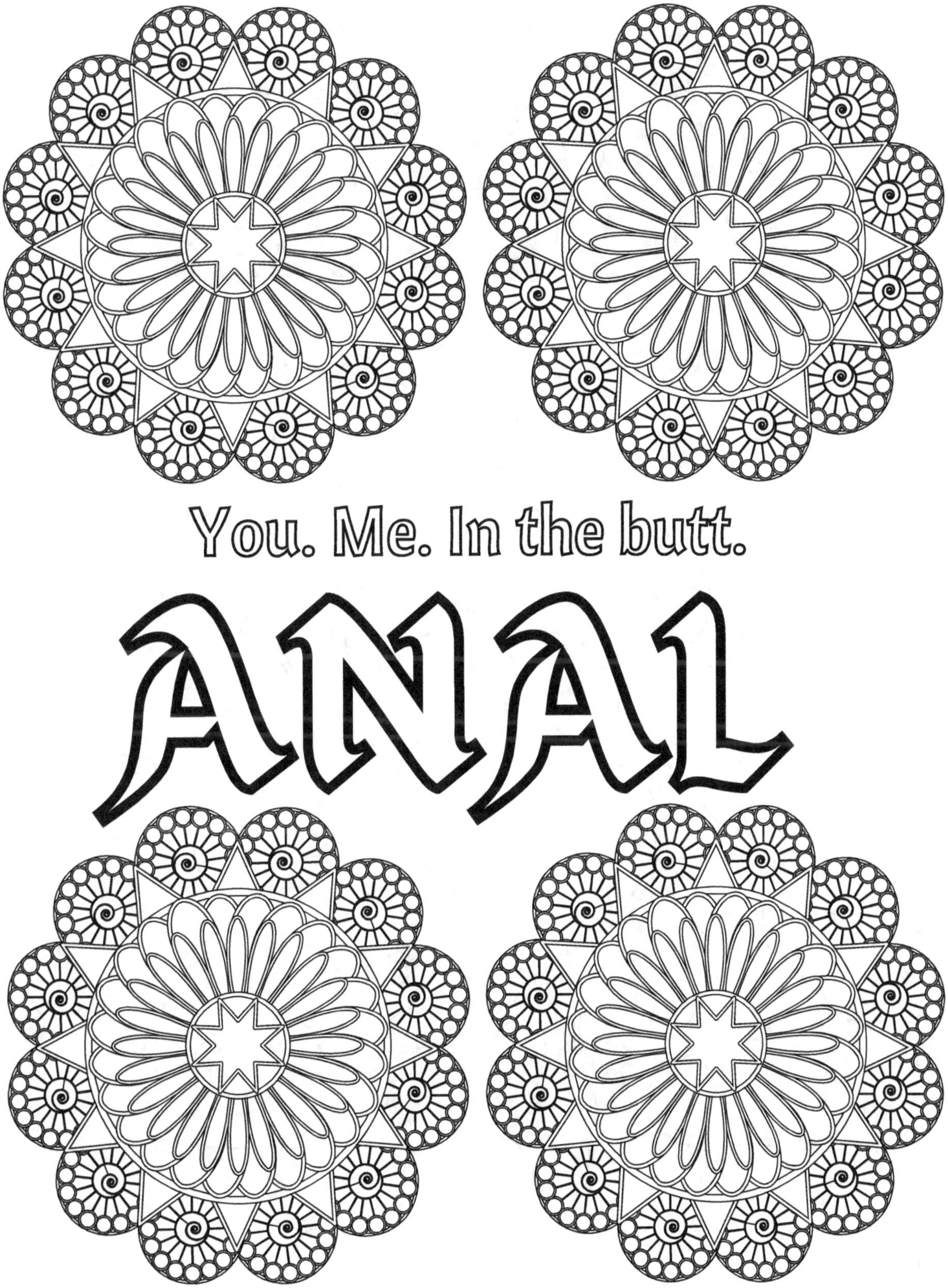

You. Me. In the butt.

ANAL

ANAL

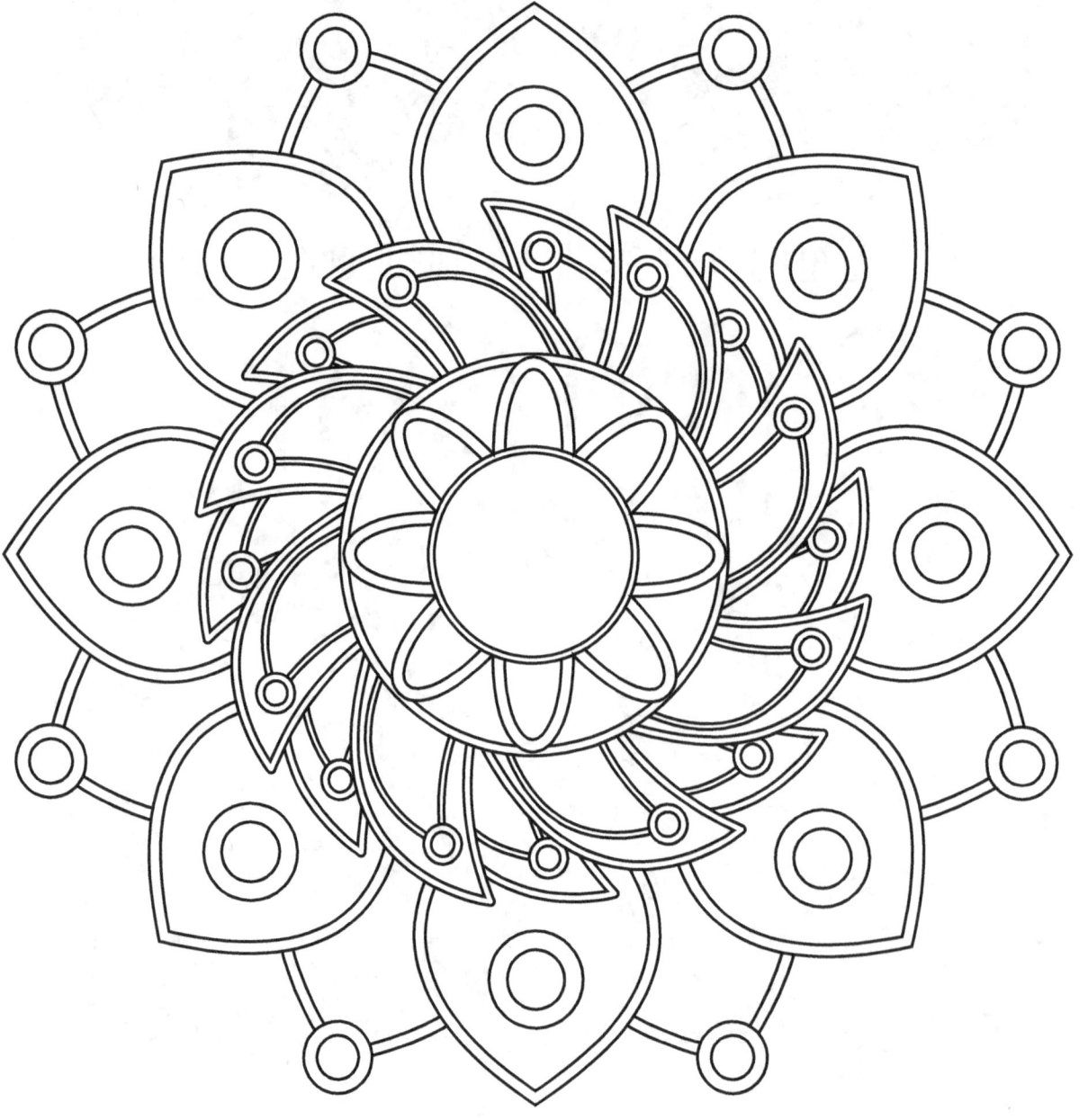

ANAL

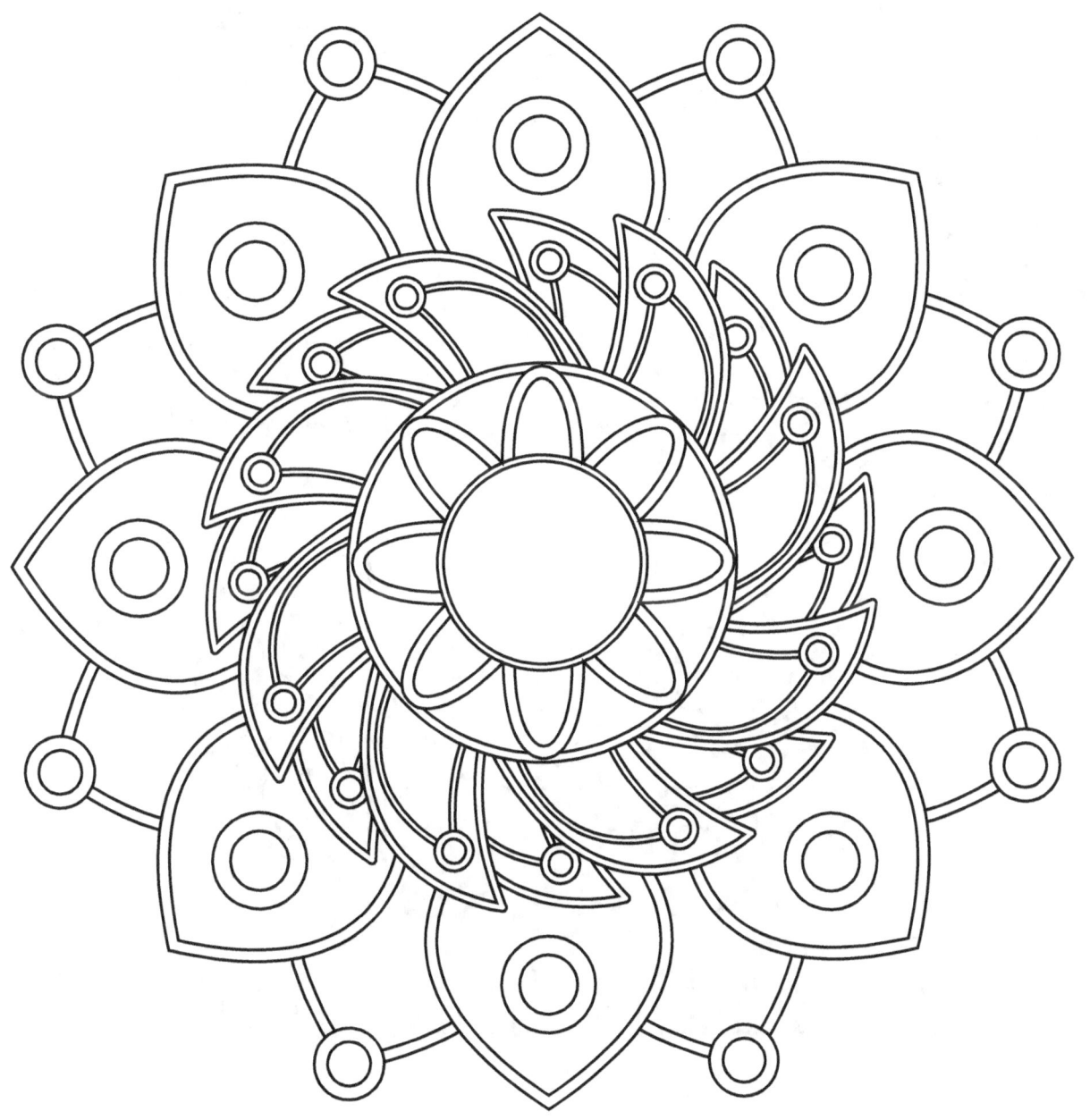

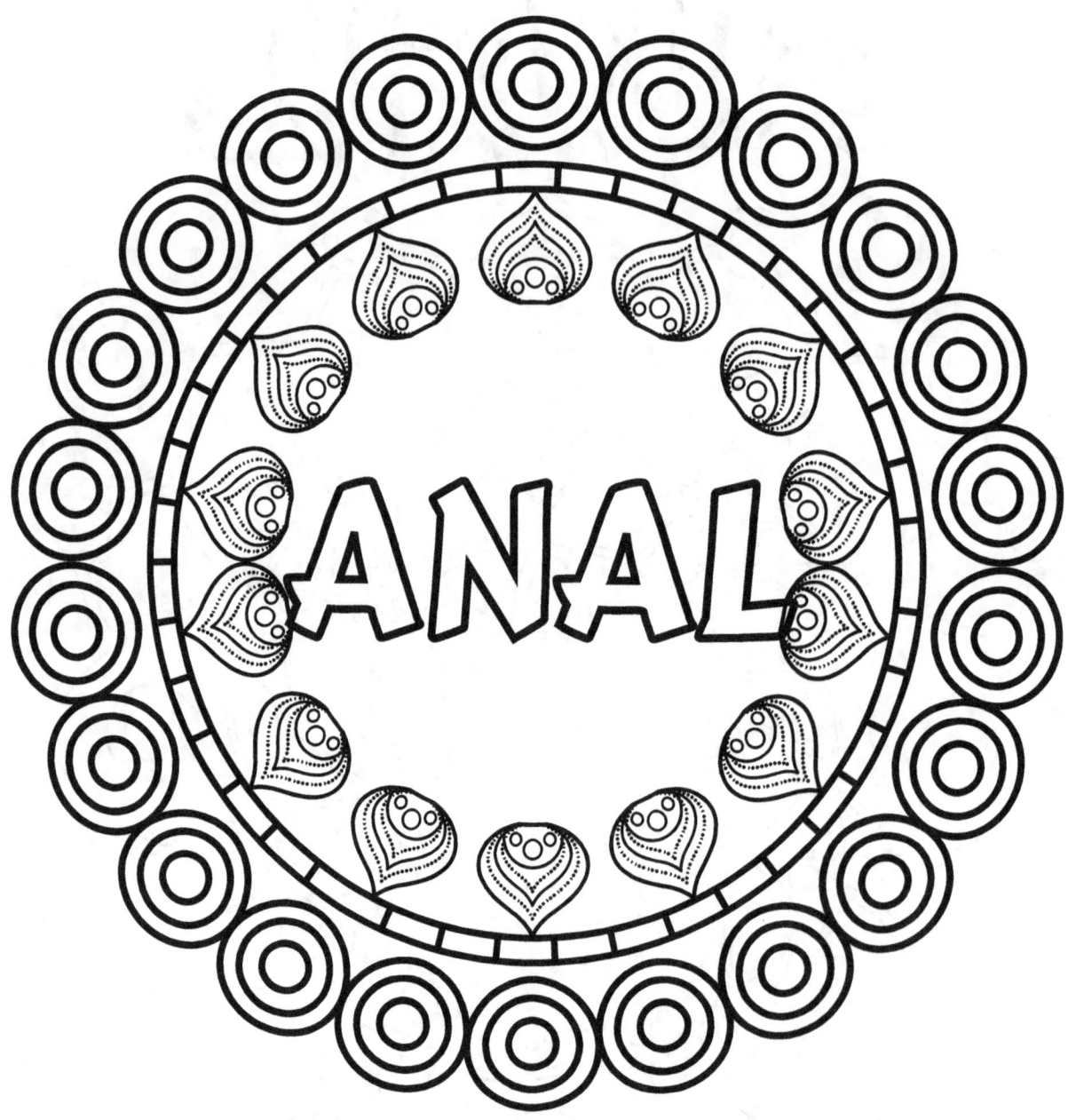

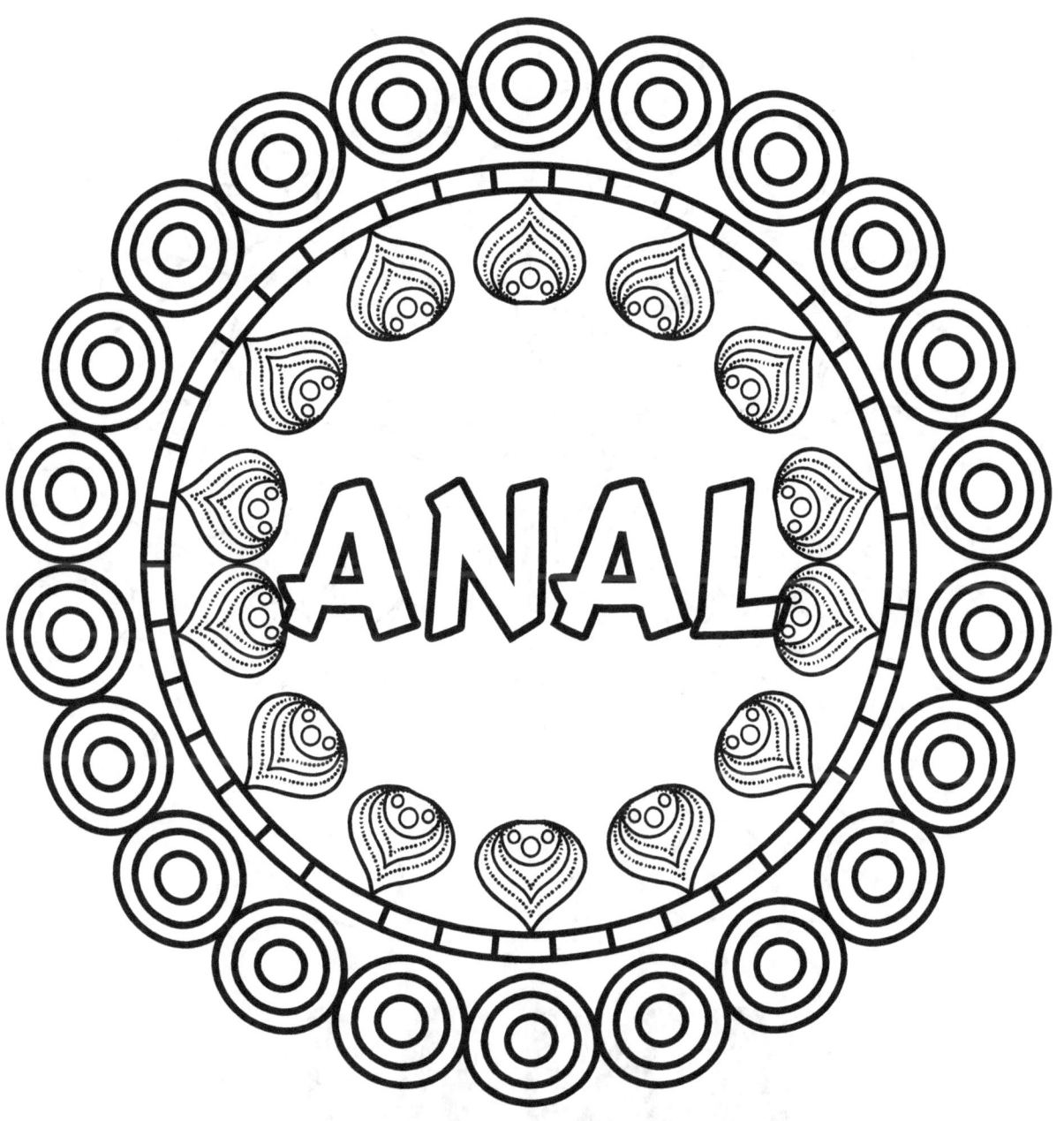

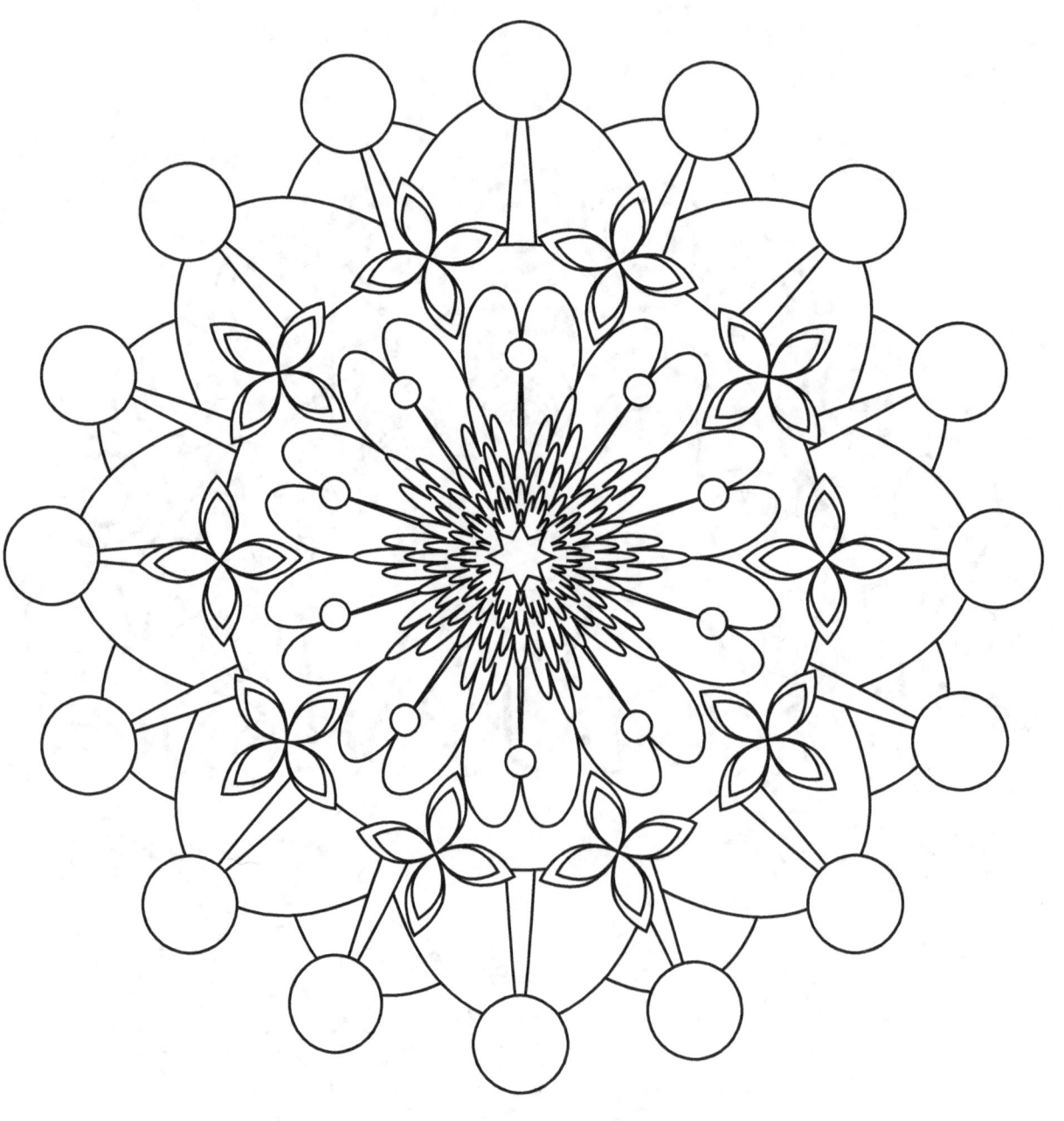

ANAL

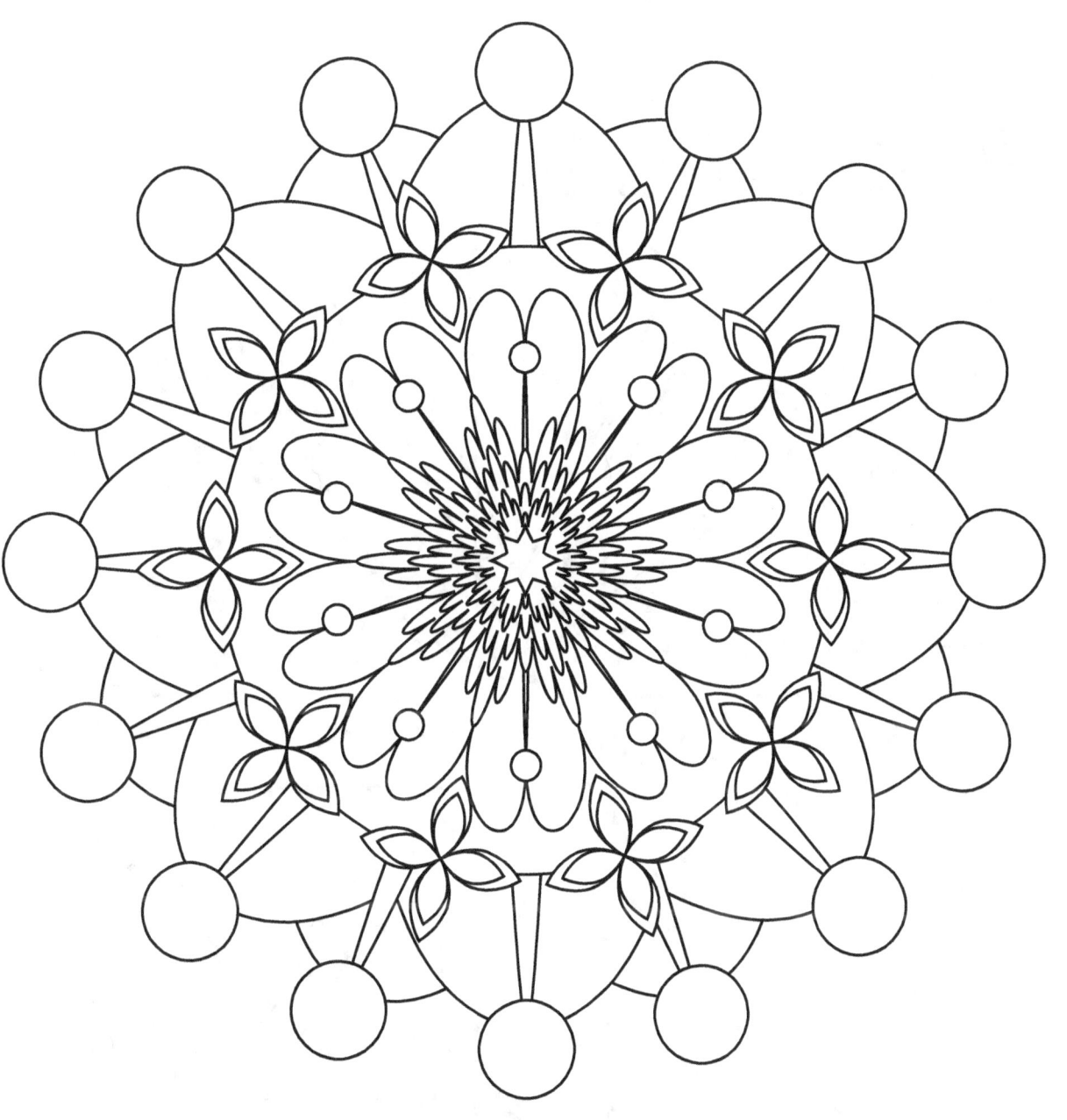

ANAL

ANAL

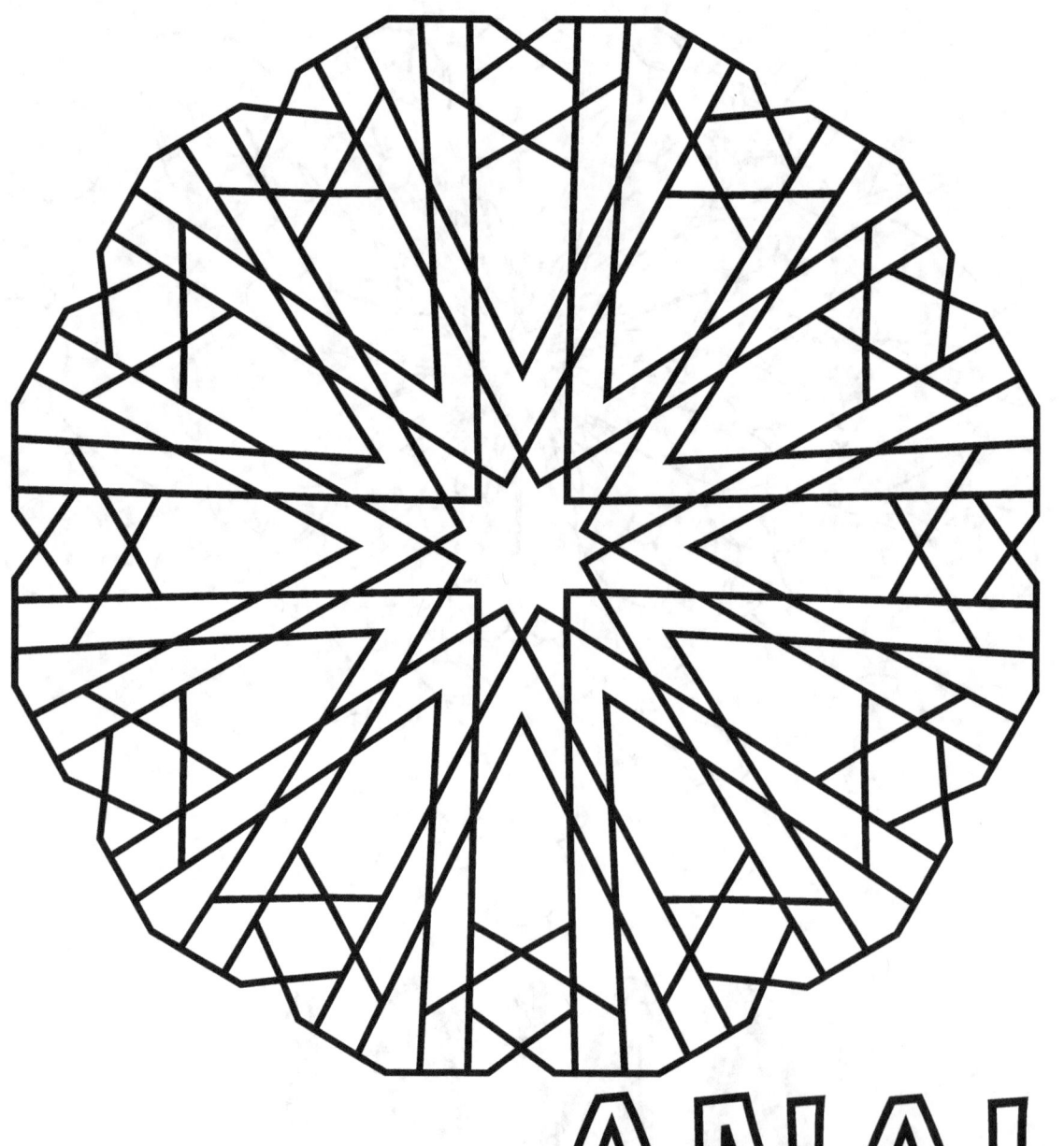

ANAL

ANAL

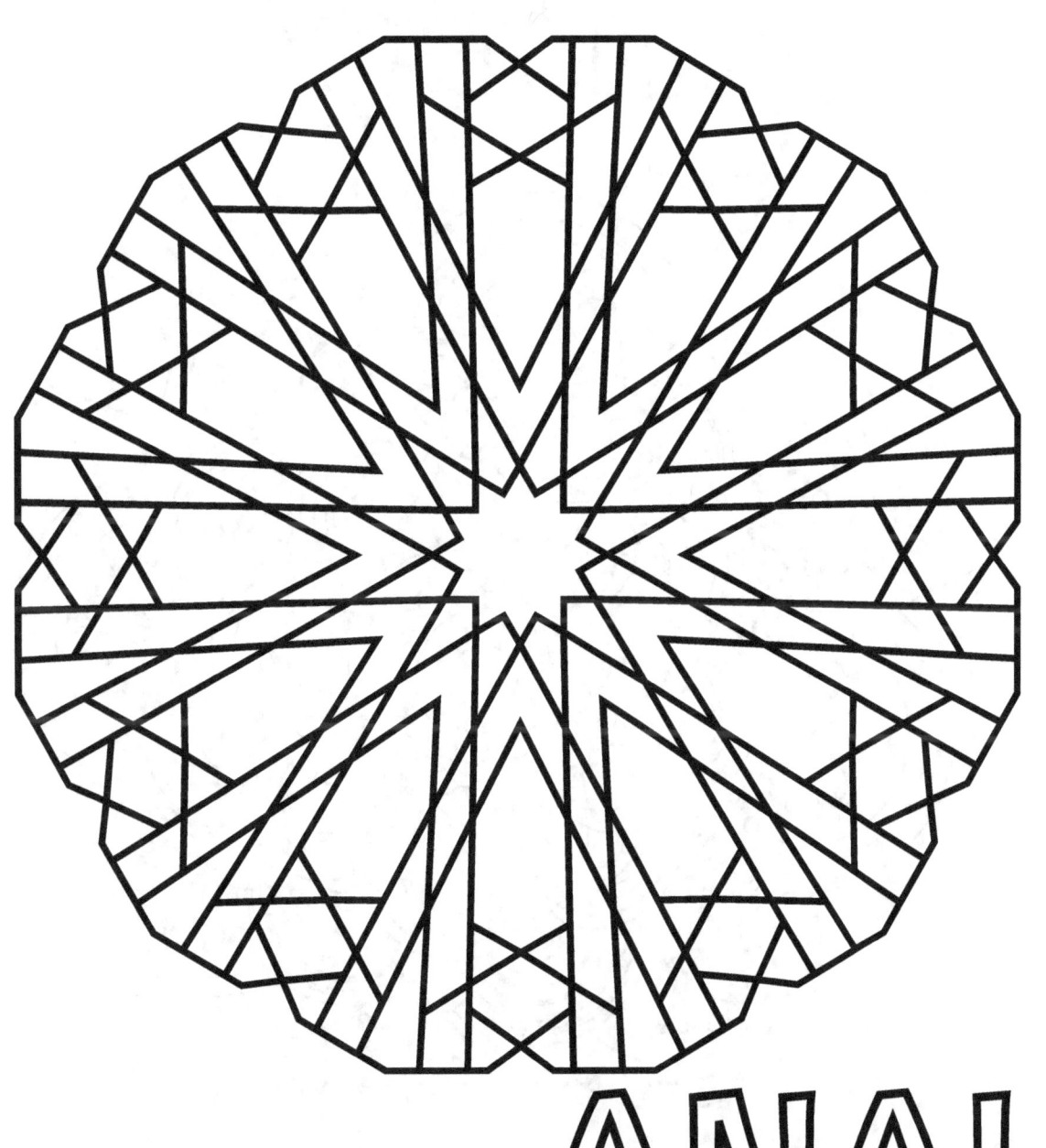

ANAL

permission to enter?

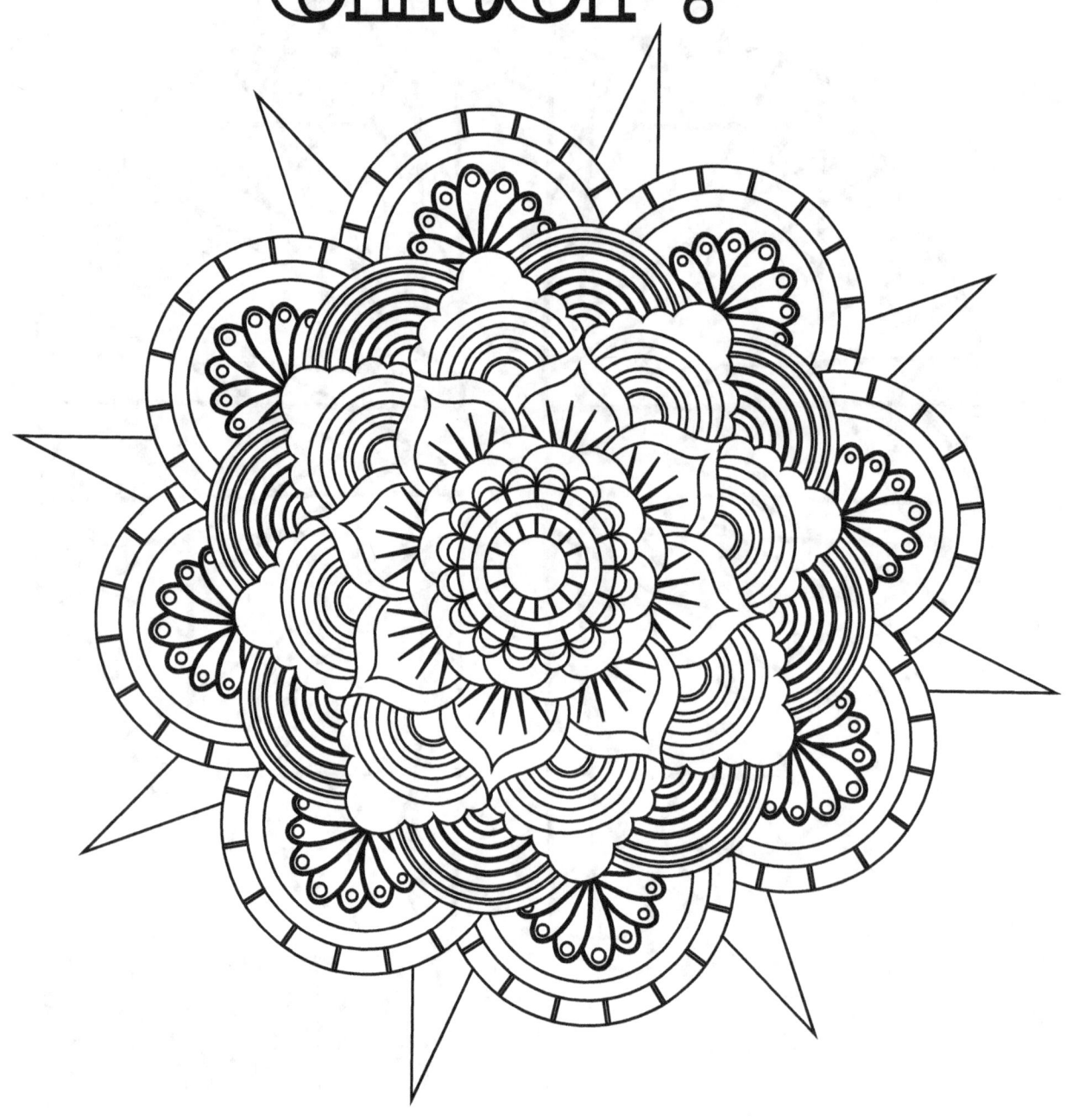

permission to enter?

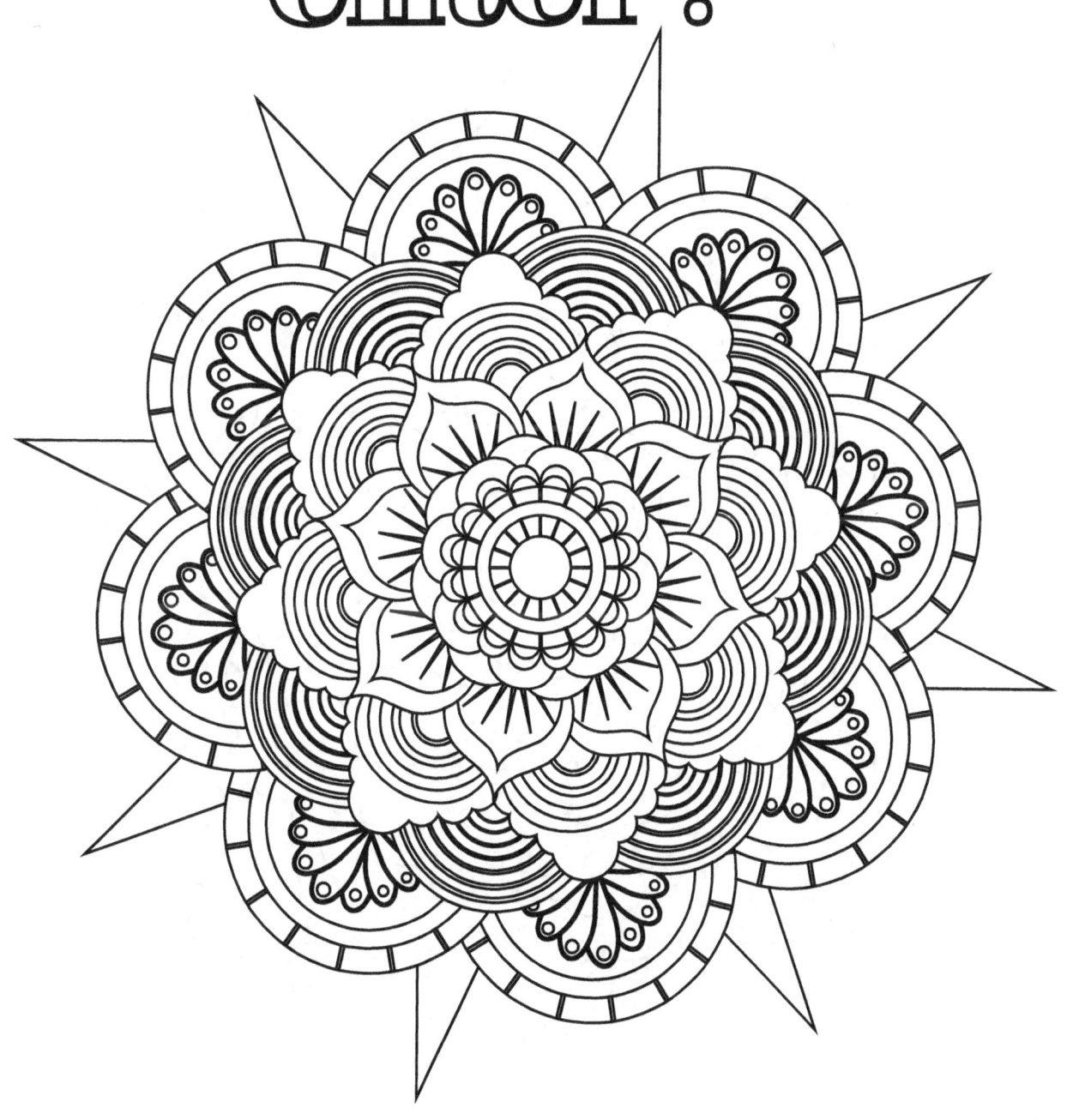

ANUS PARTY!

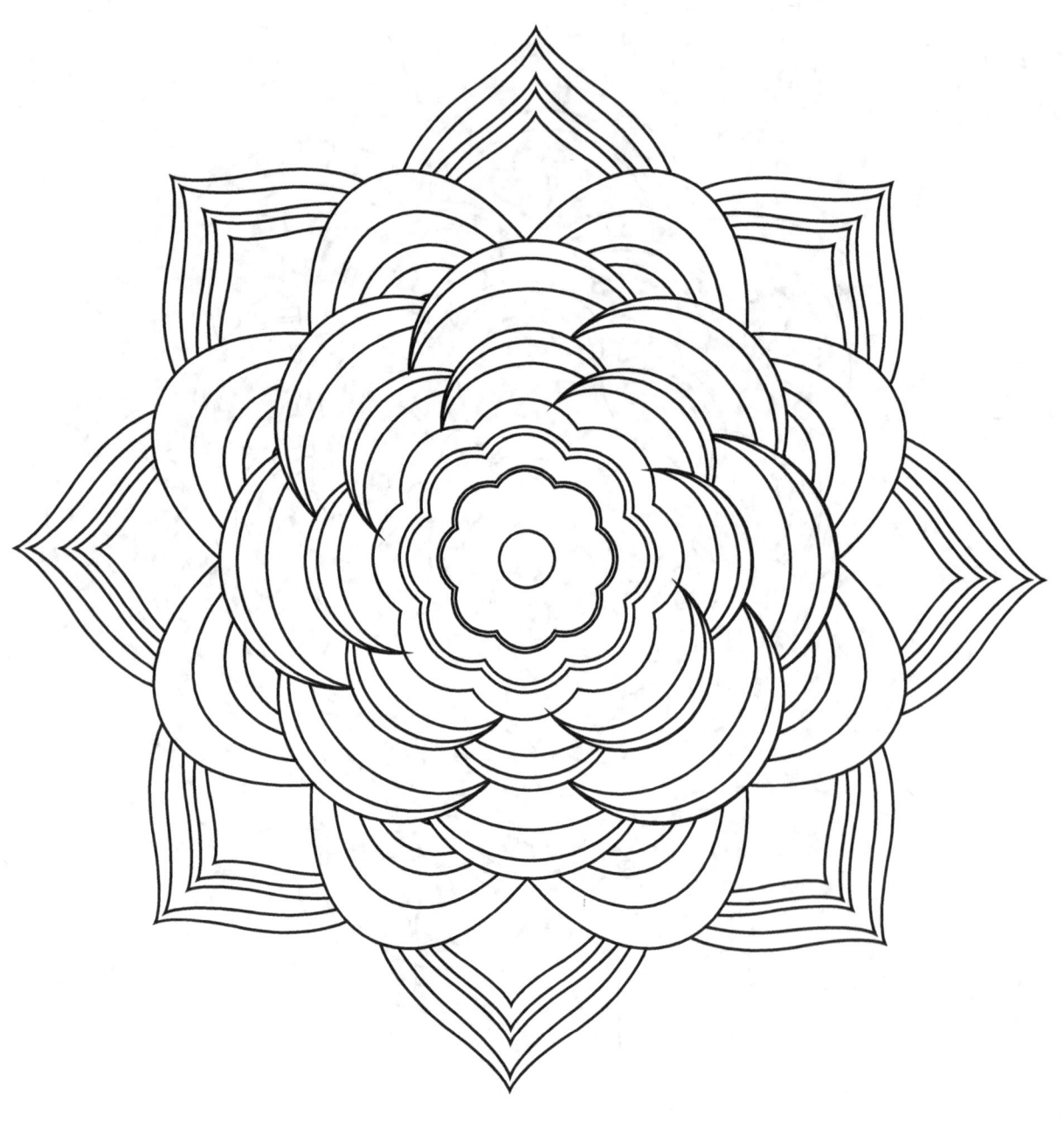

ANUS PARTY!

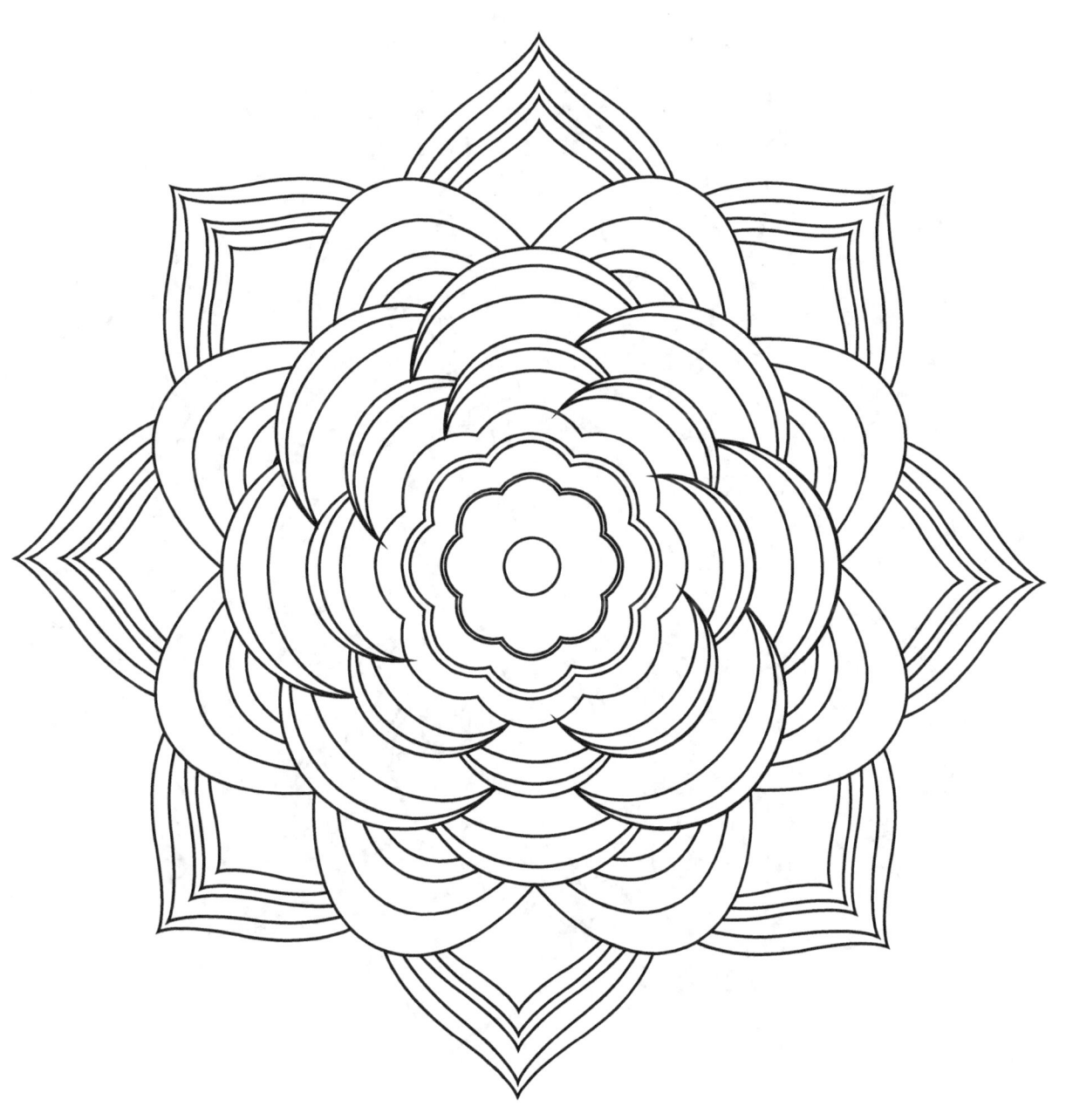

ANAL

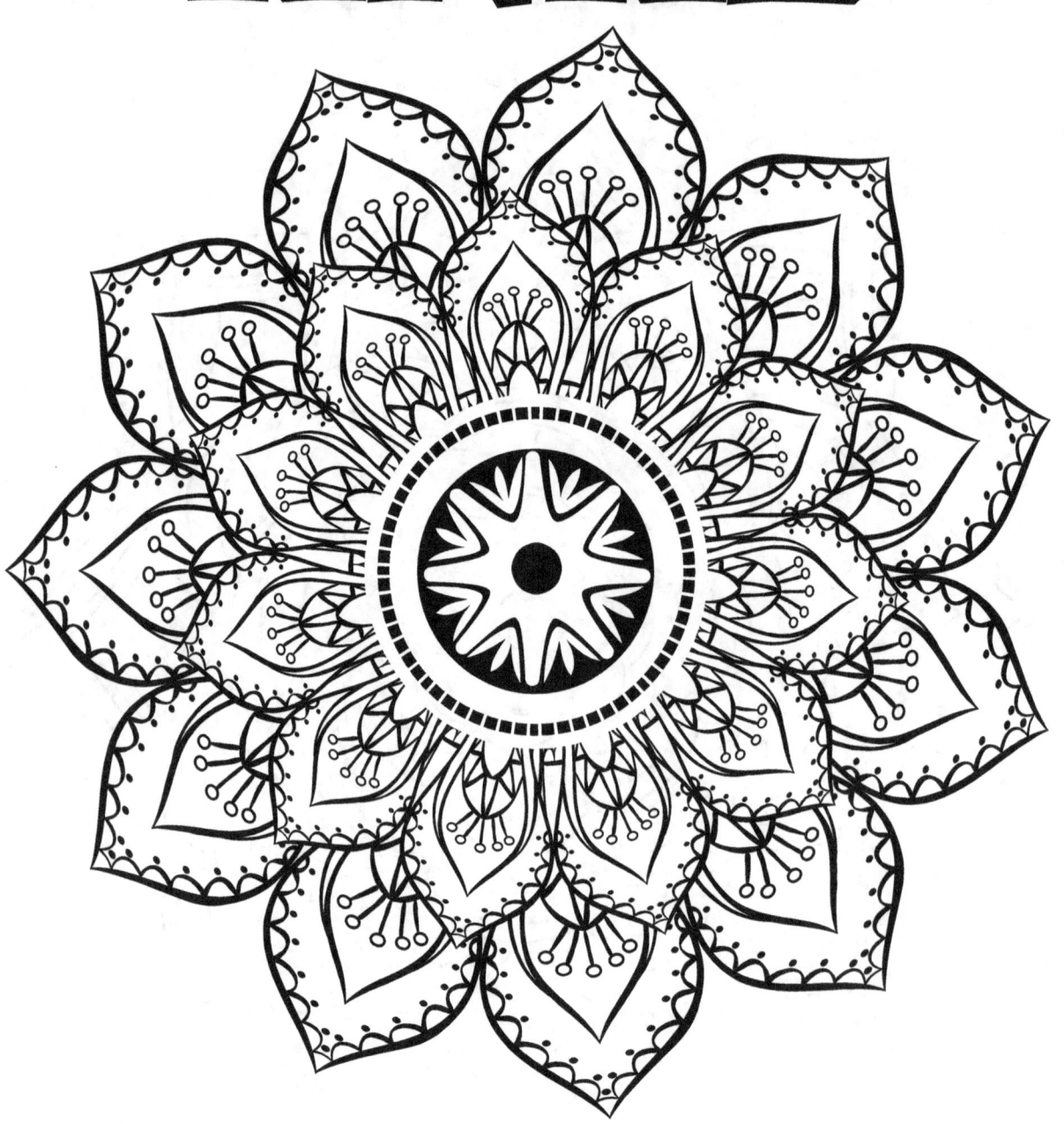

ANAL

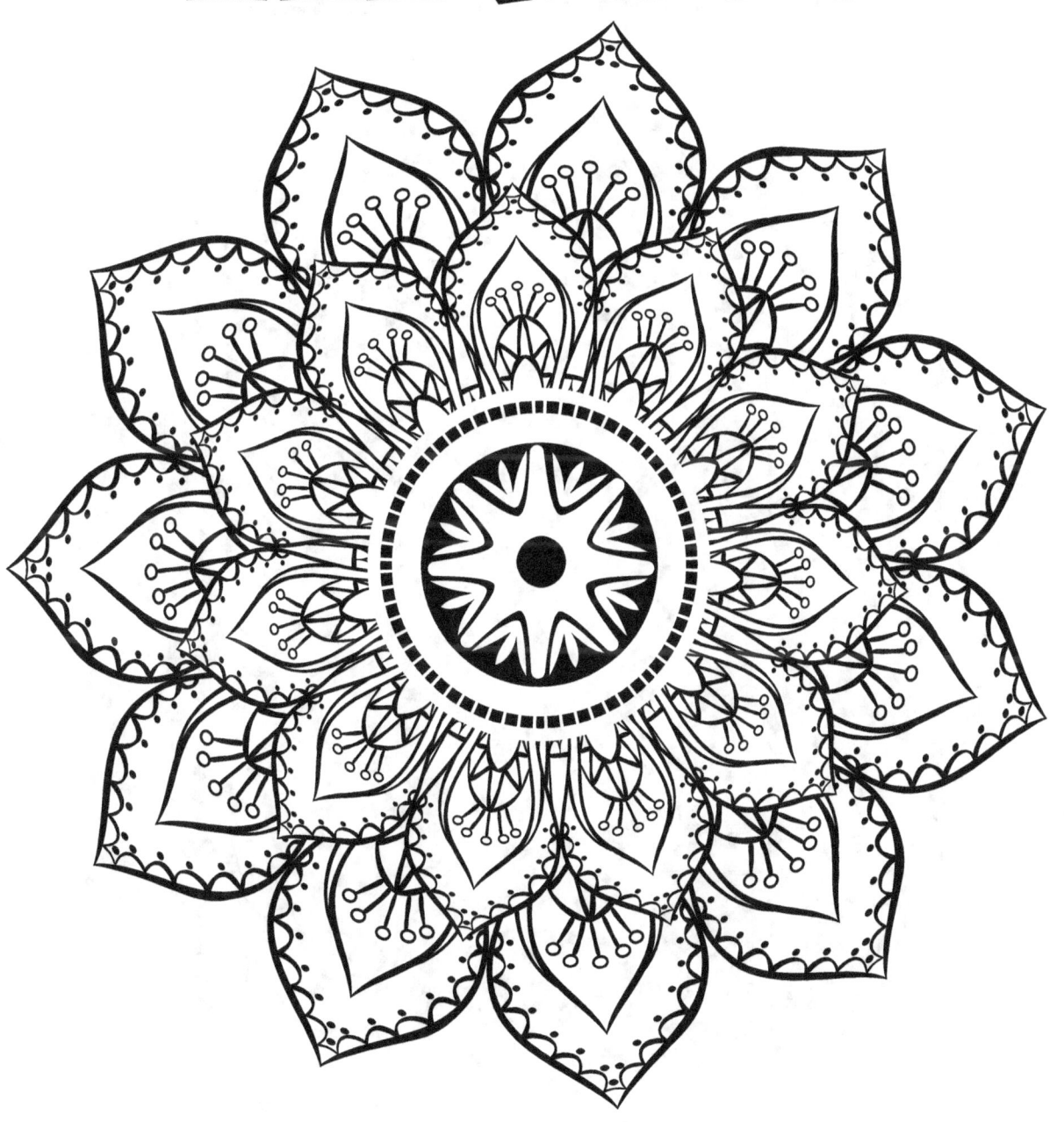

ANAL

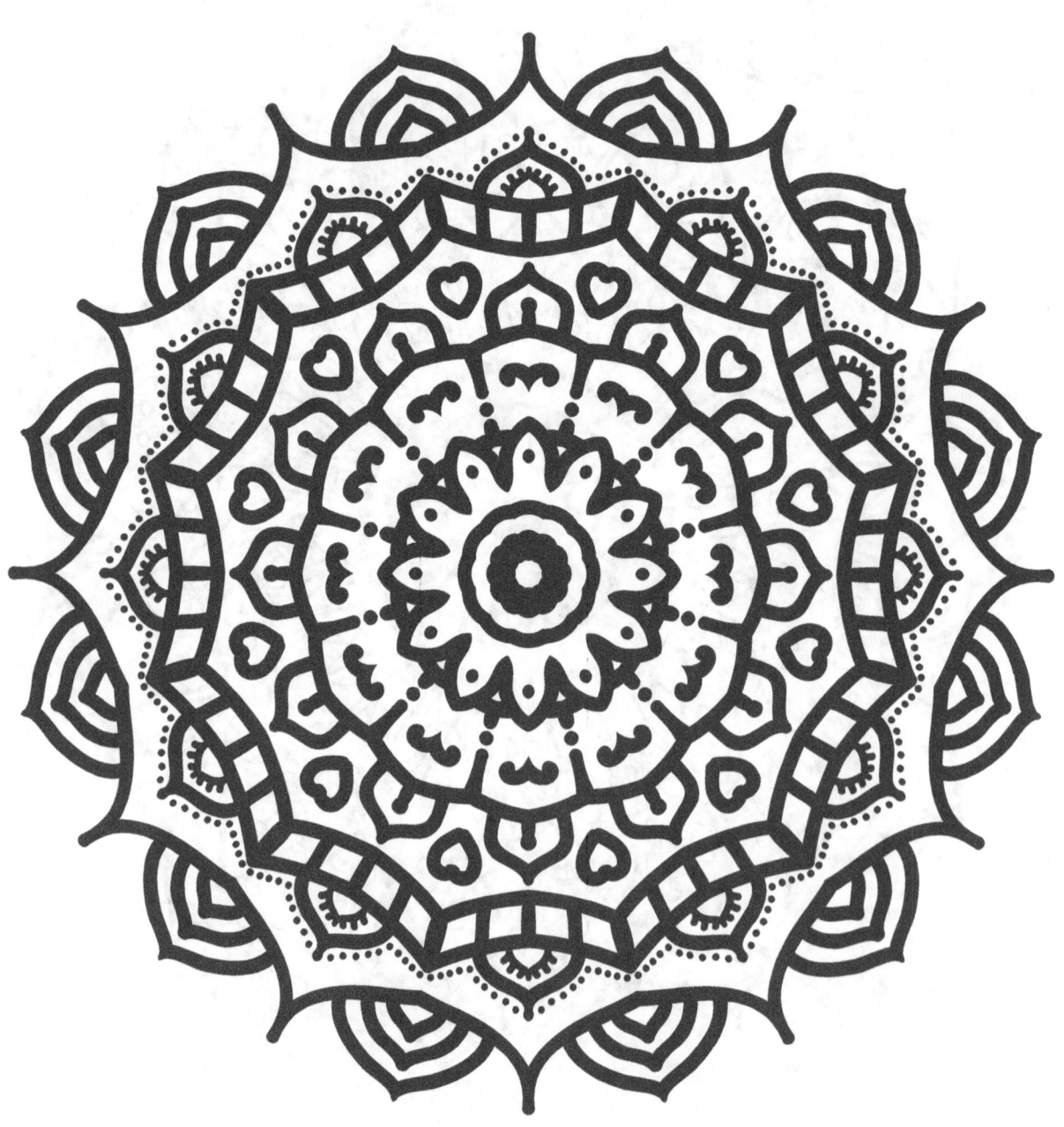

ANAL

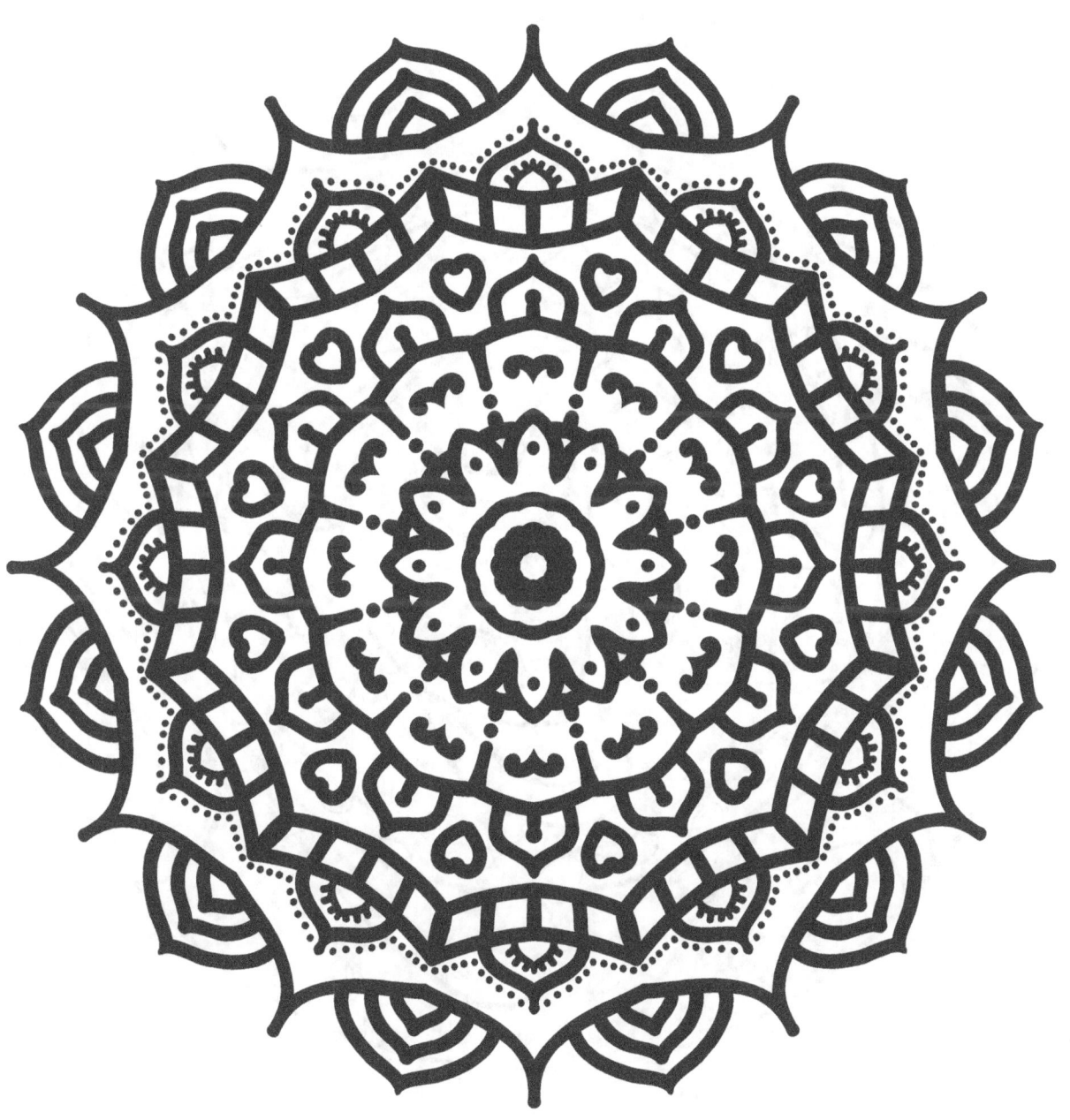

back door

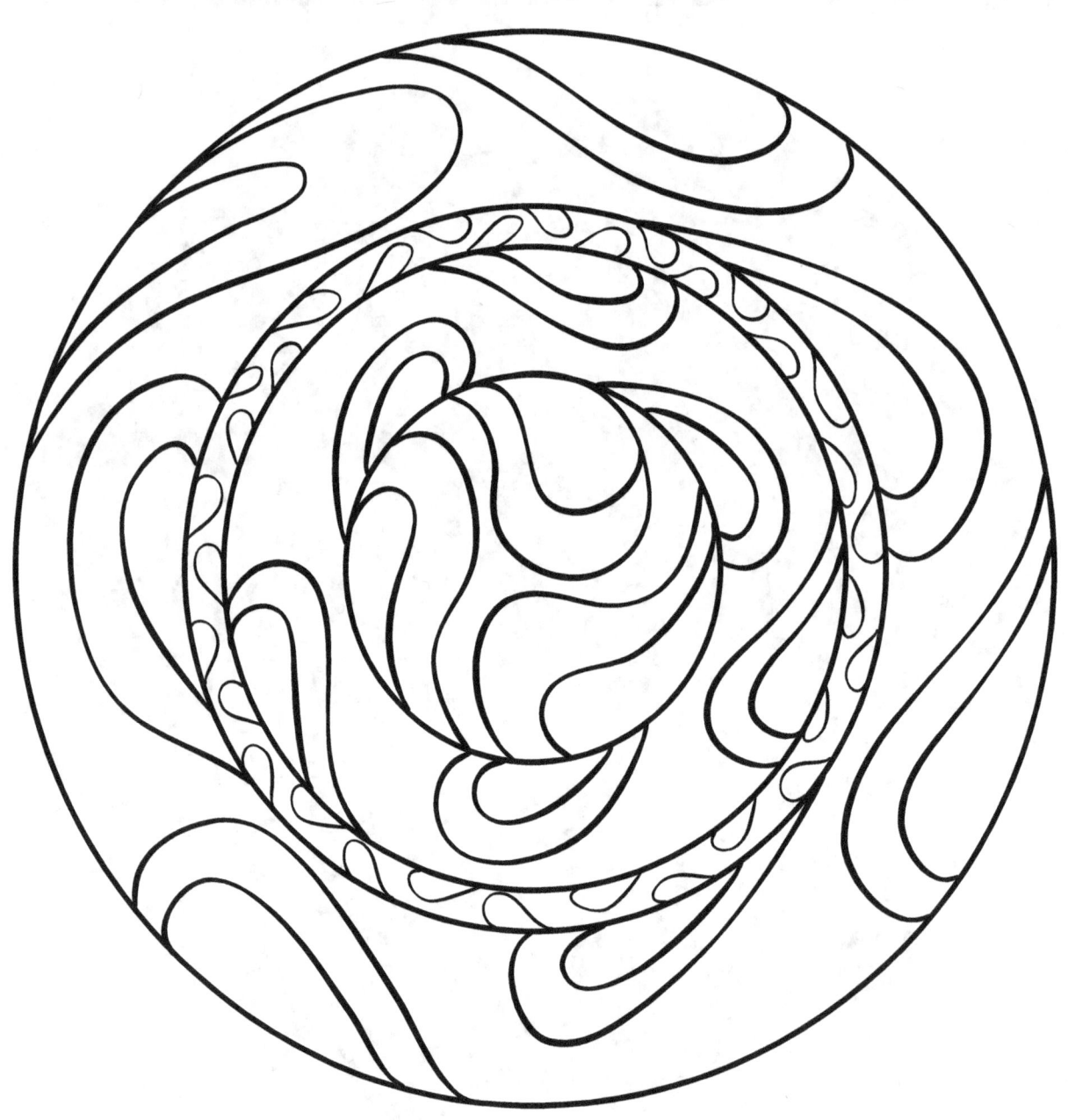

back door

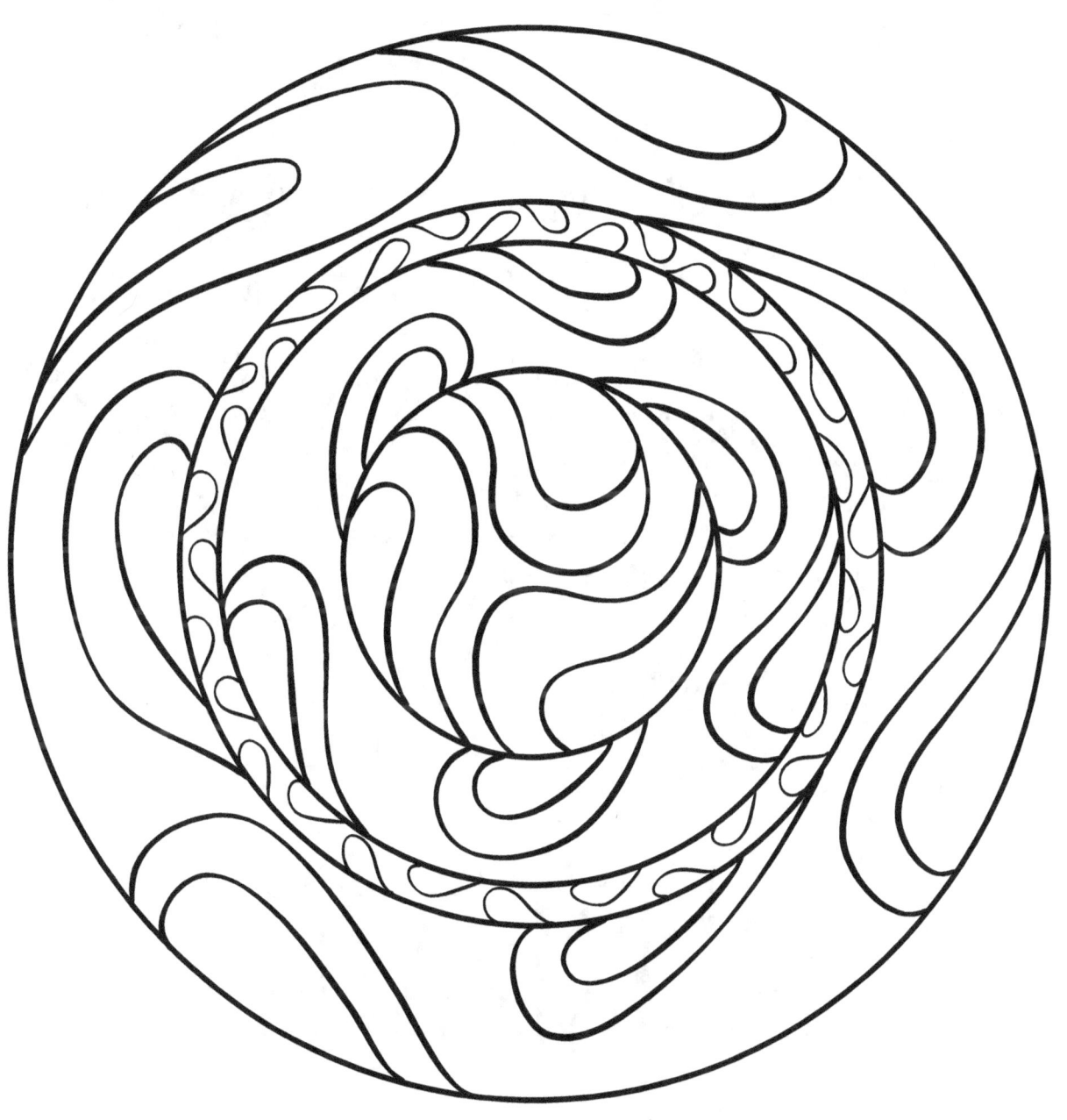

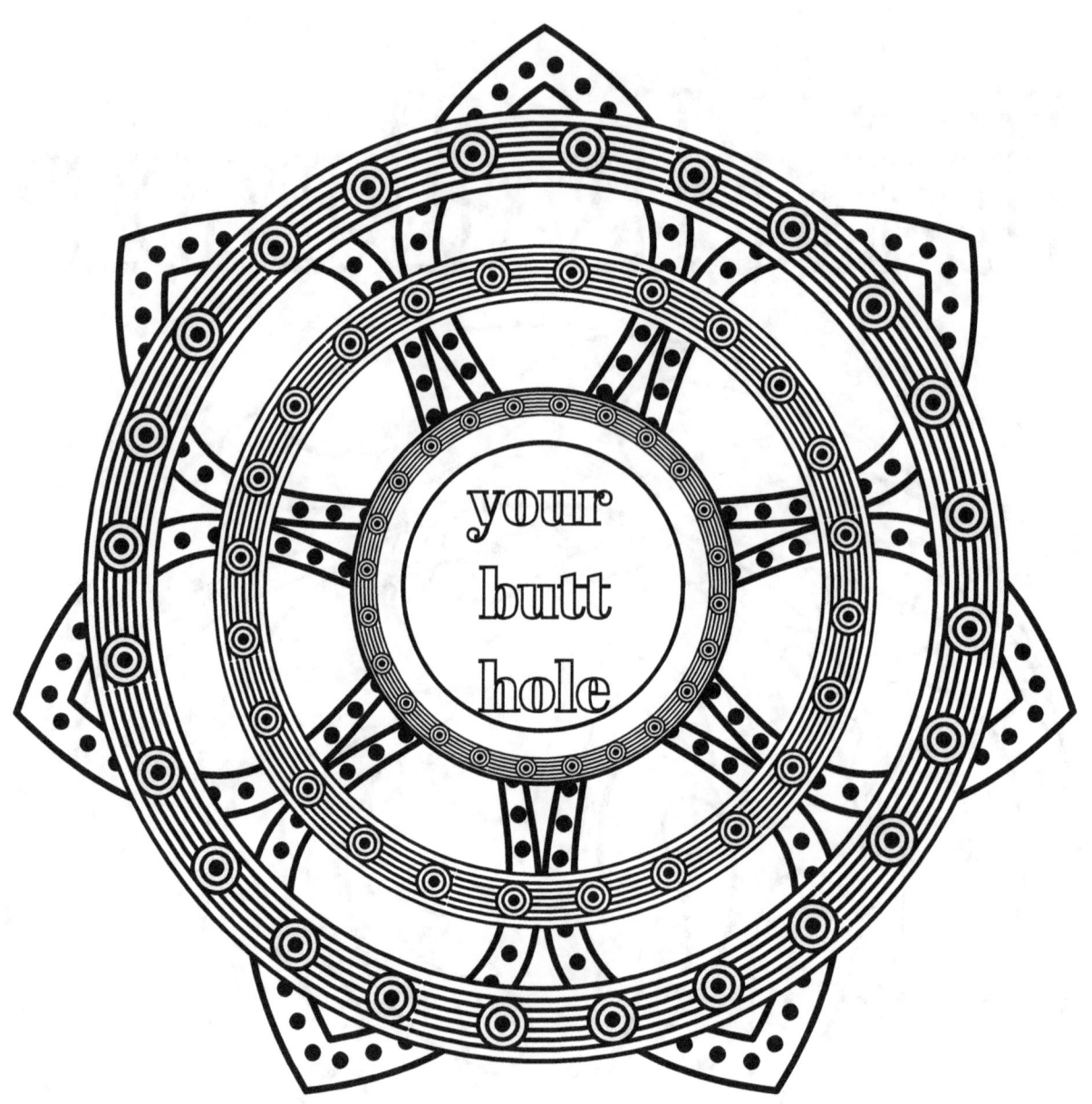

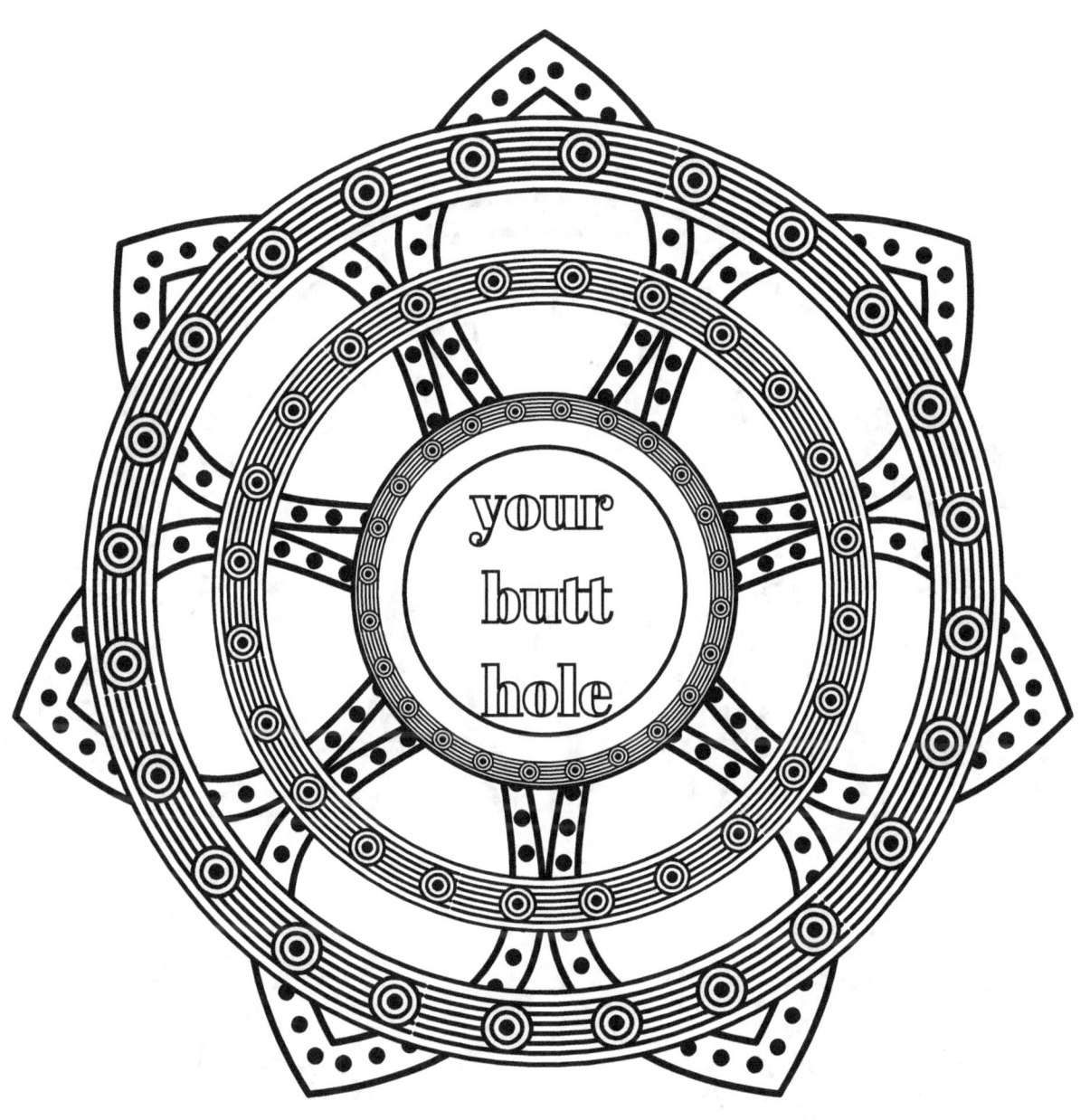

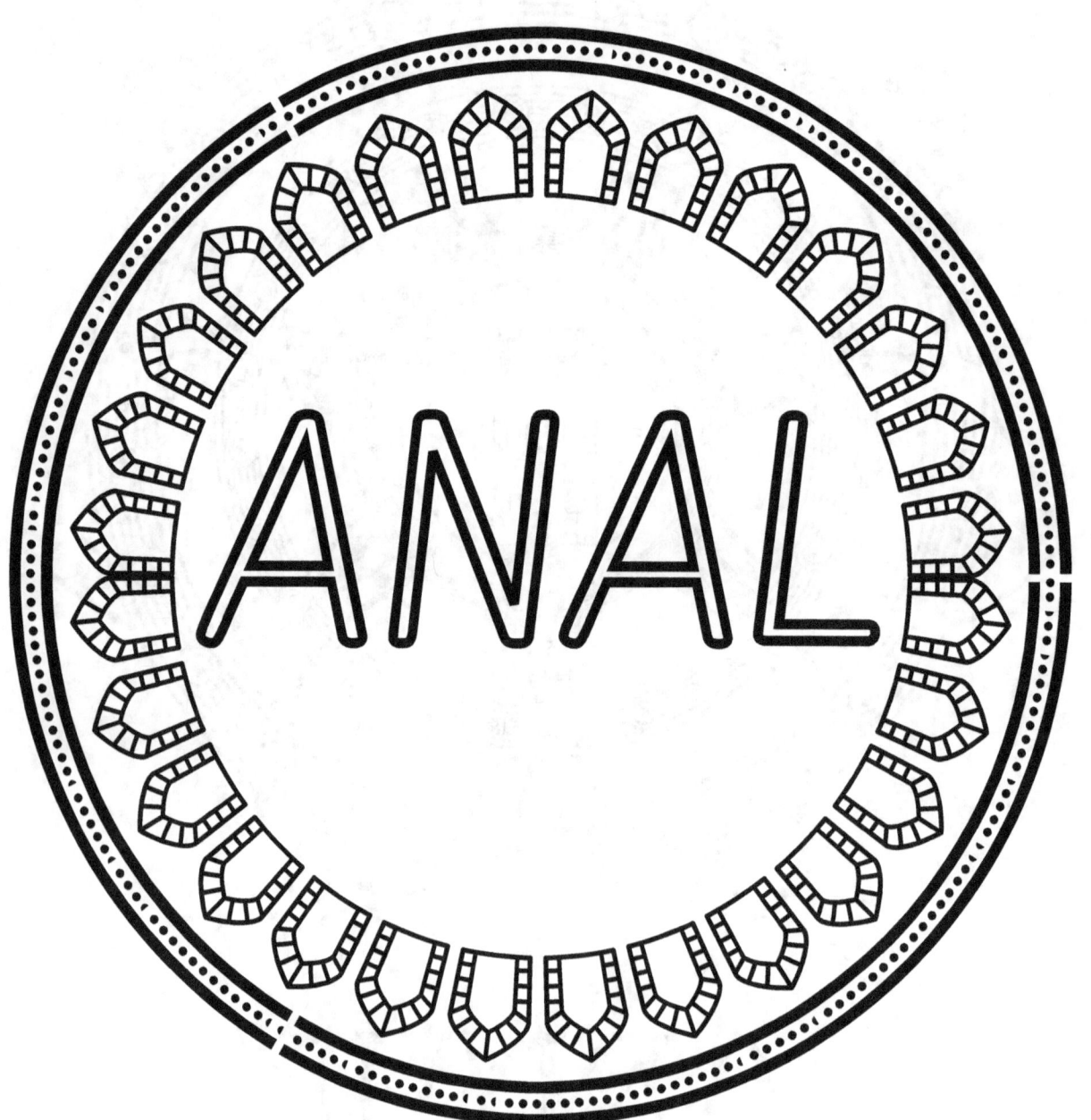

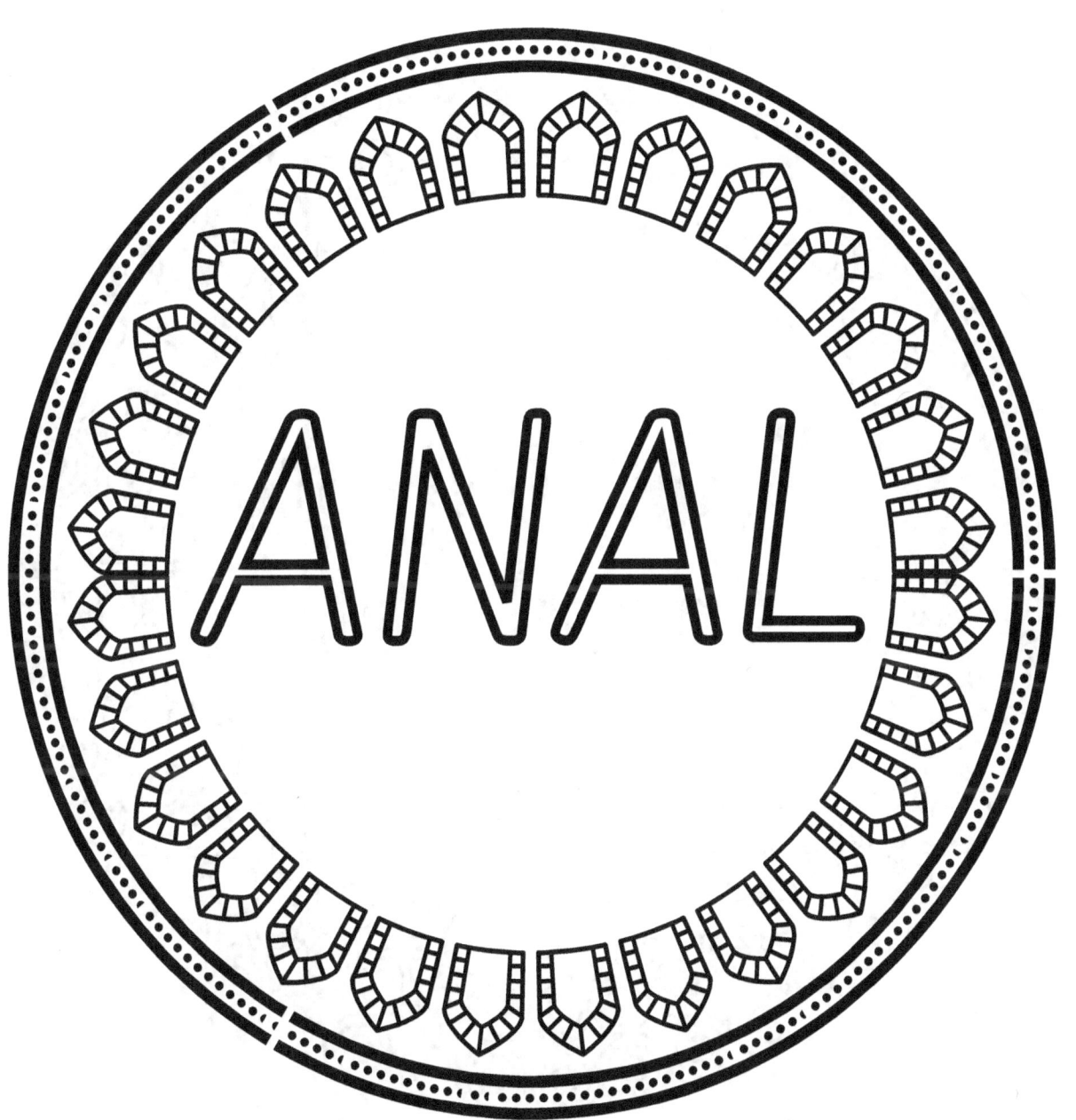

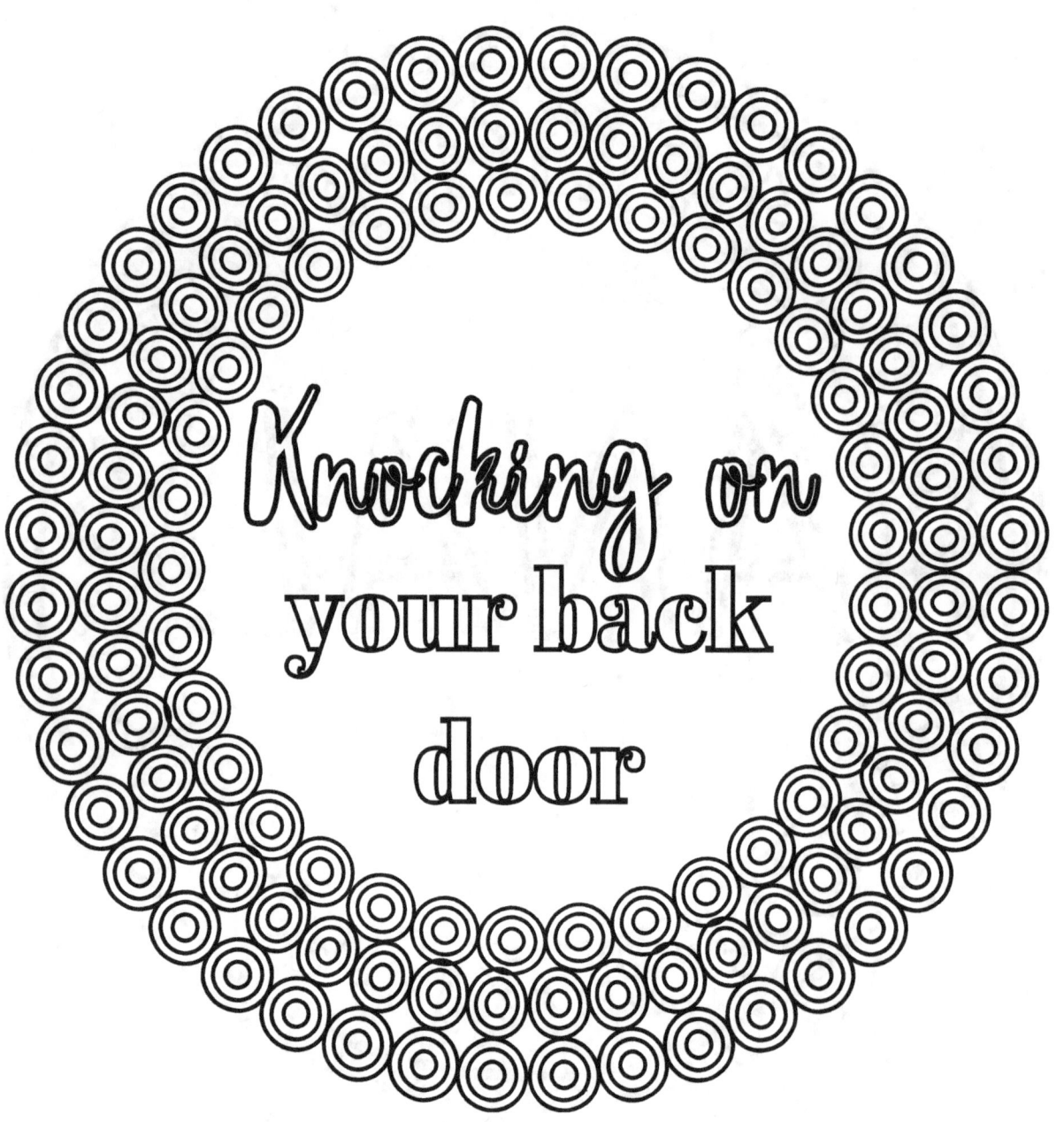

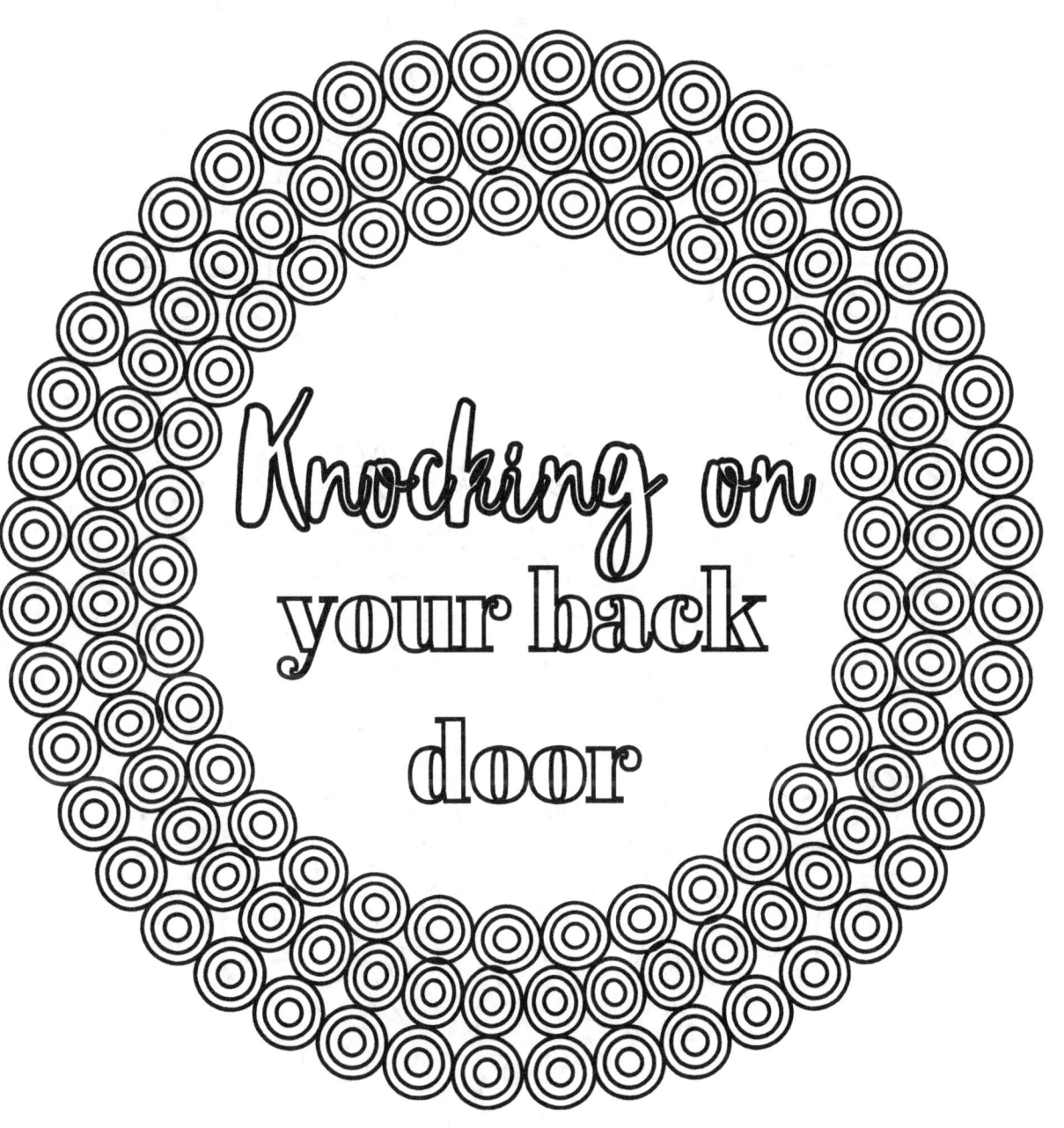

up in that

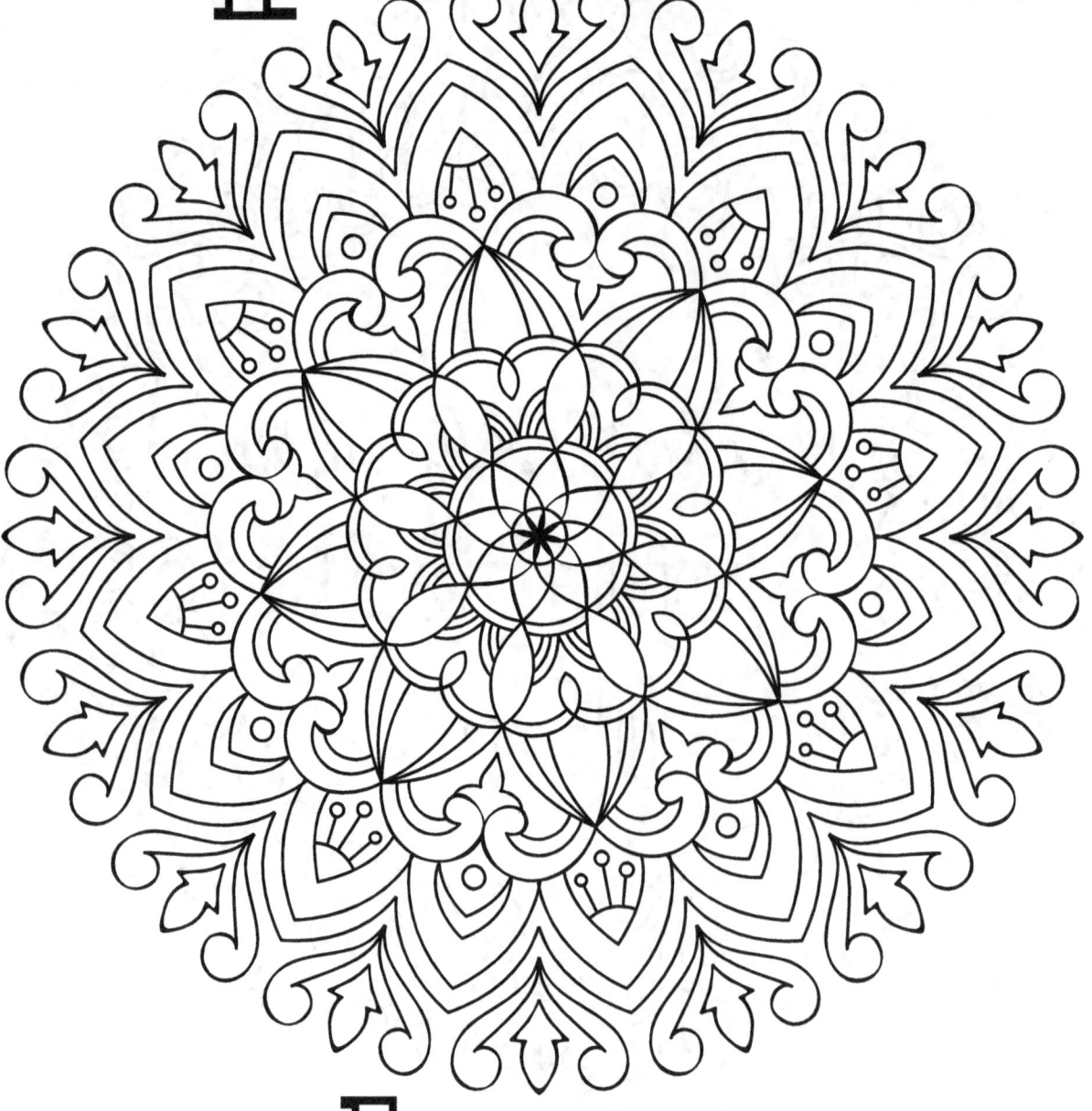

butt

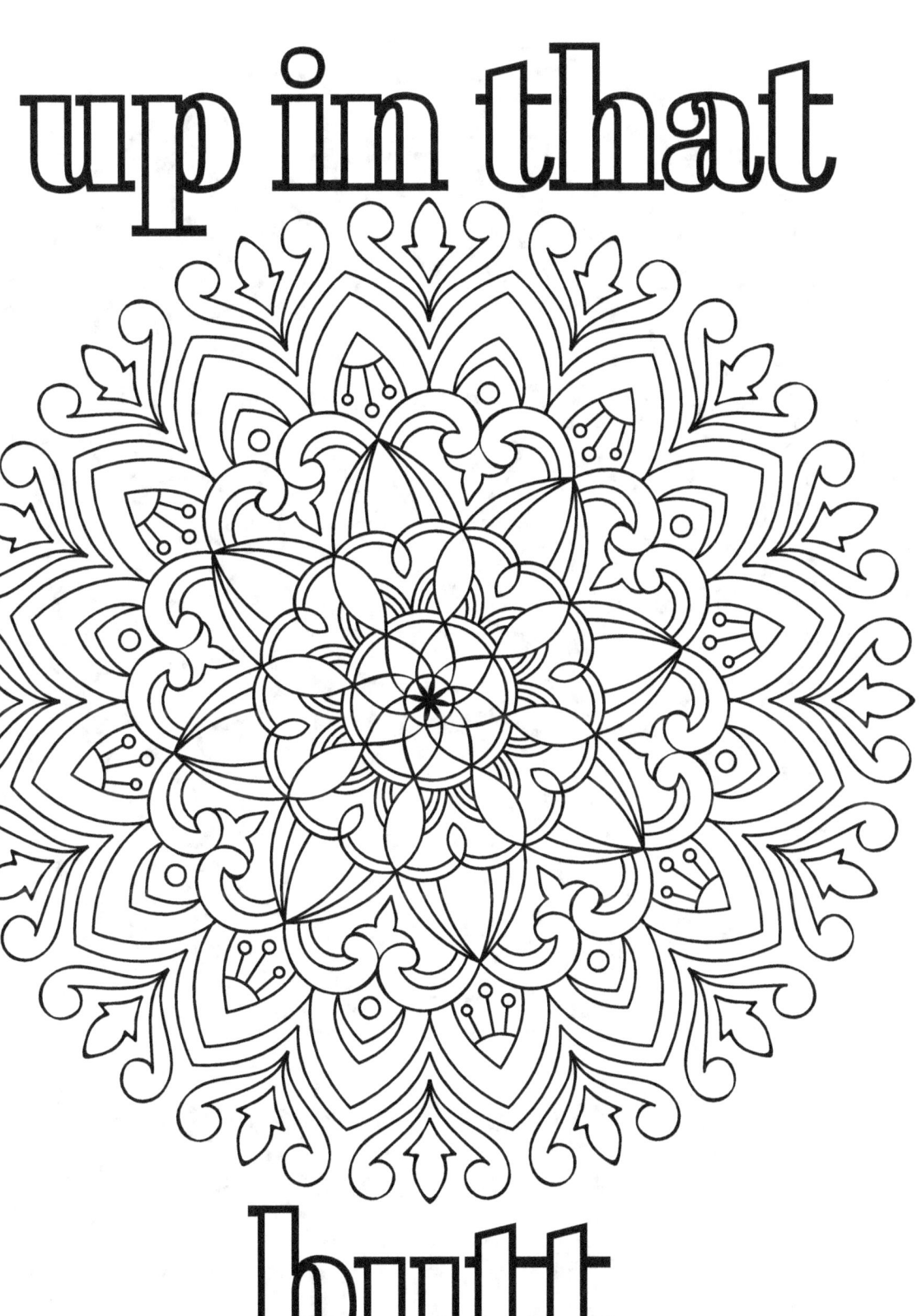

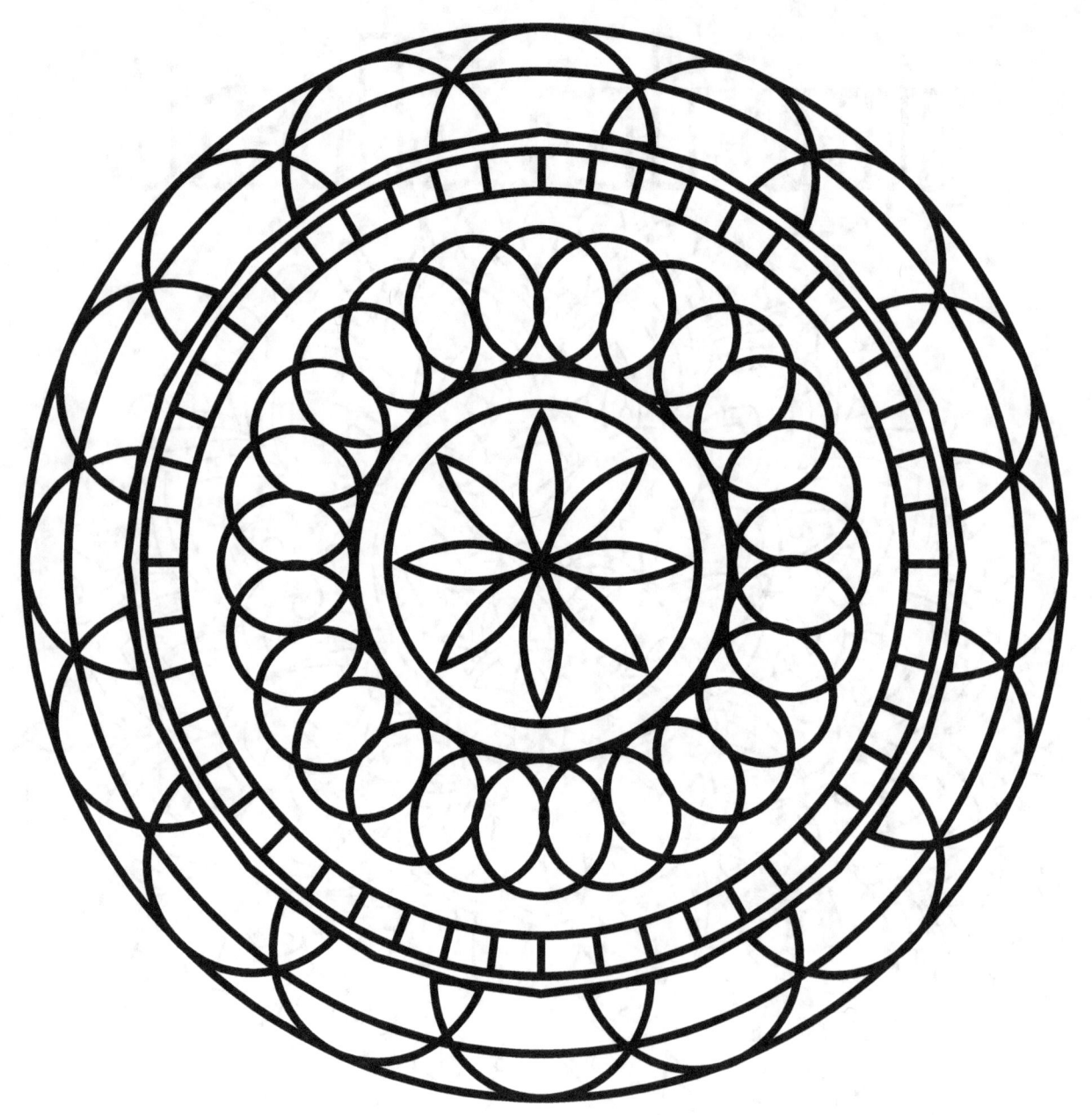

what what!
doing it in the butt!

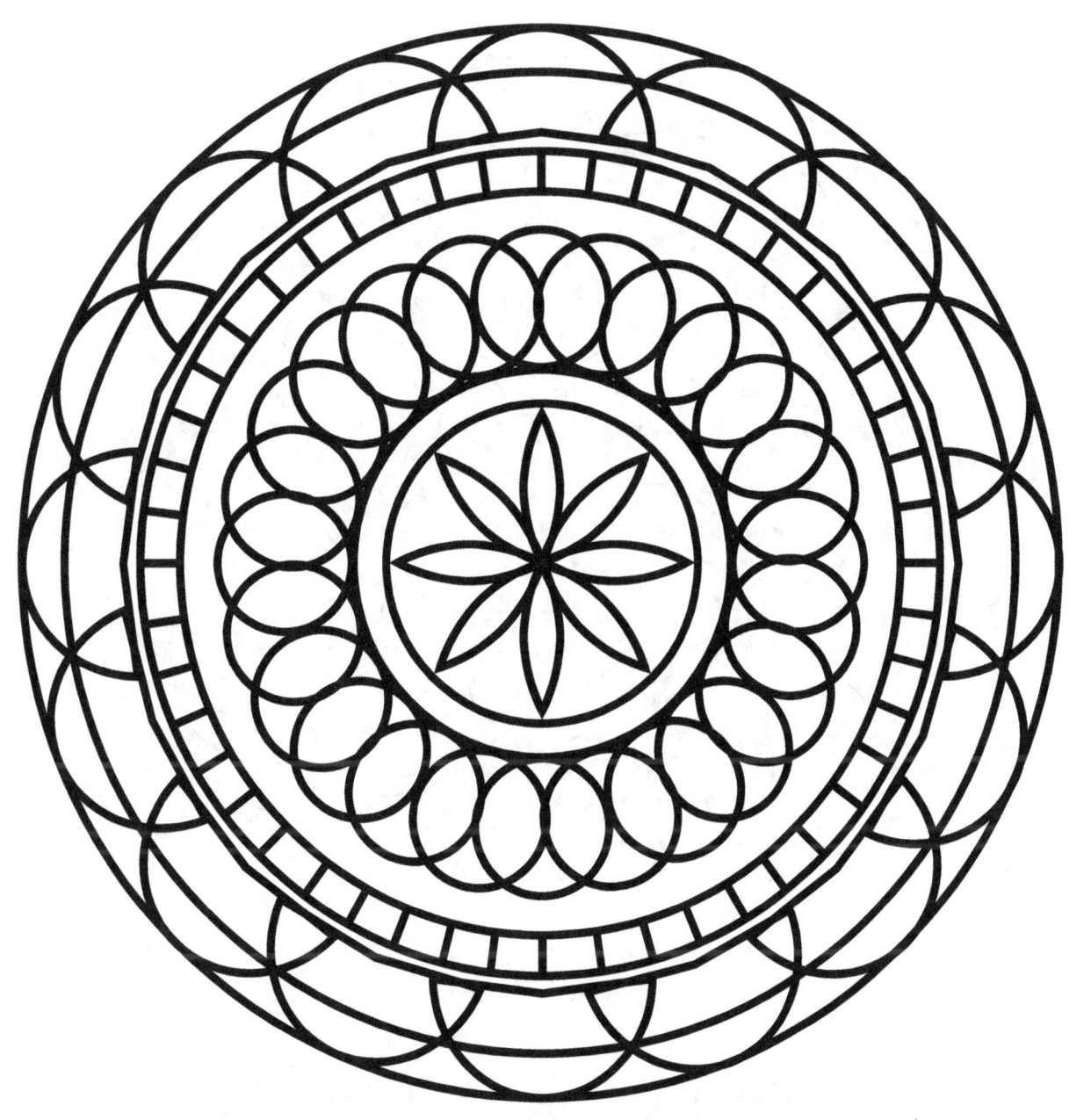

what what!
doing it in the butt!

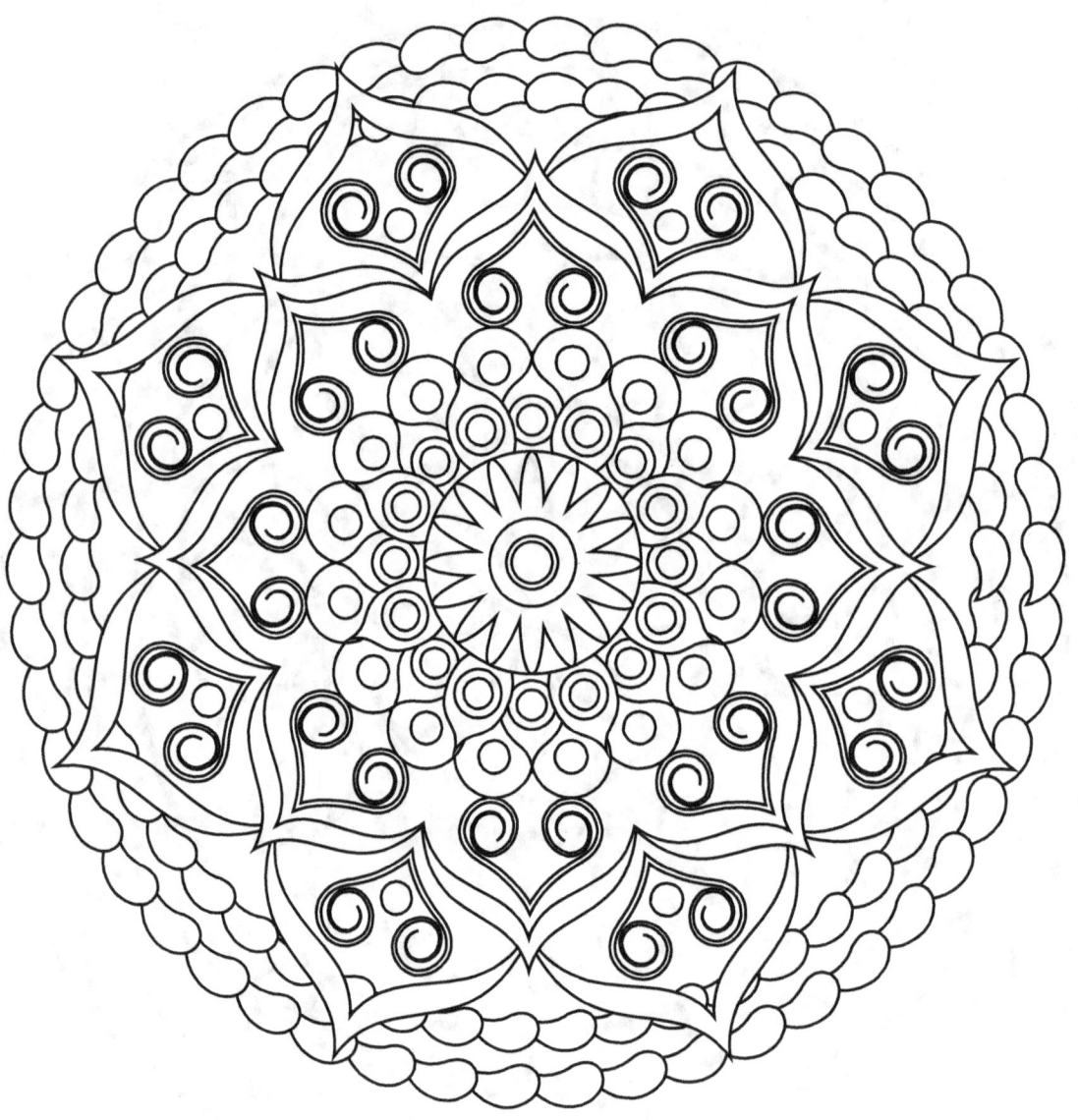

this is a booty call...for anal.

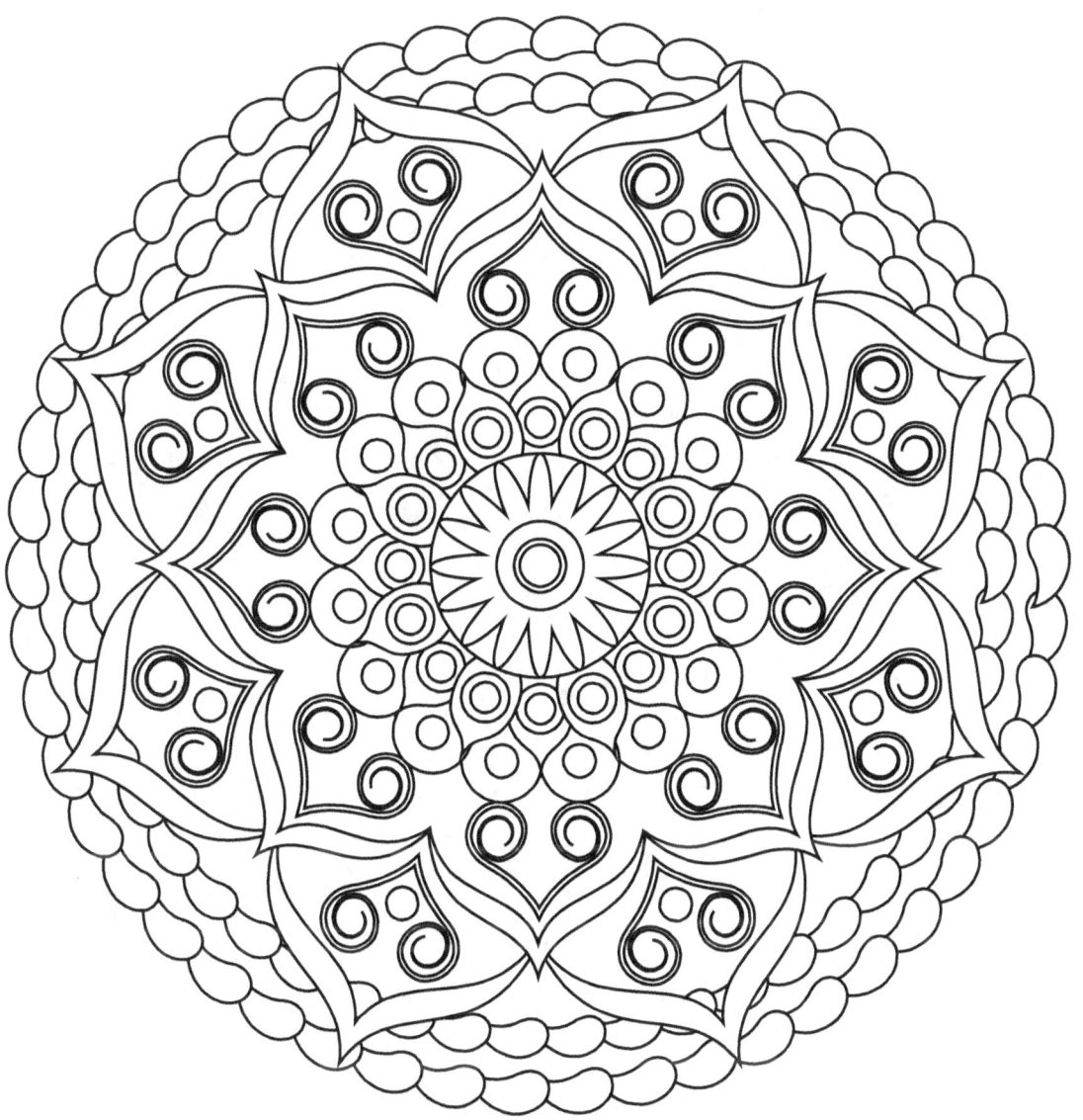

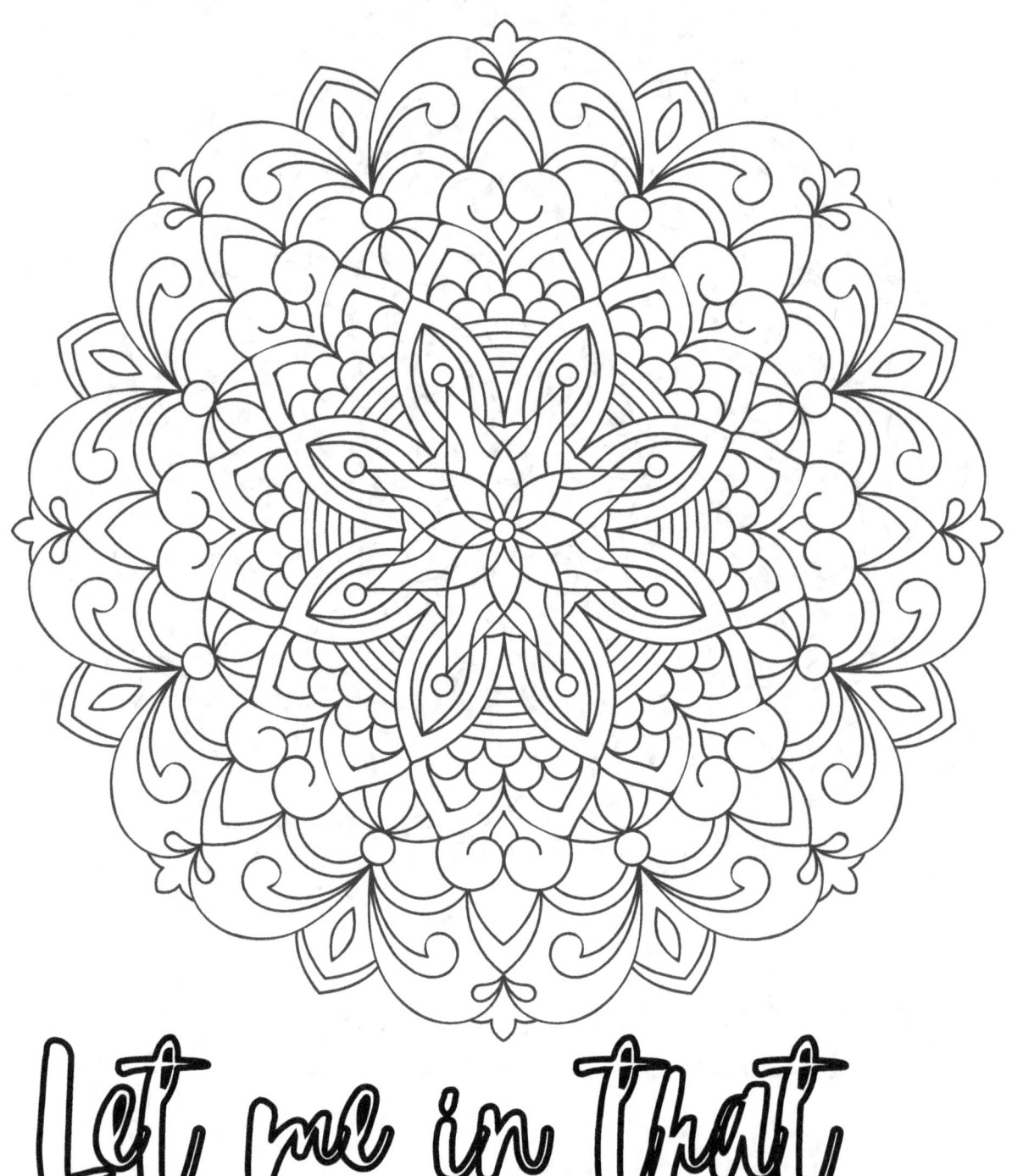

Let me in that butthole?

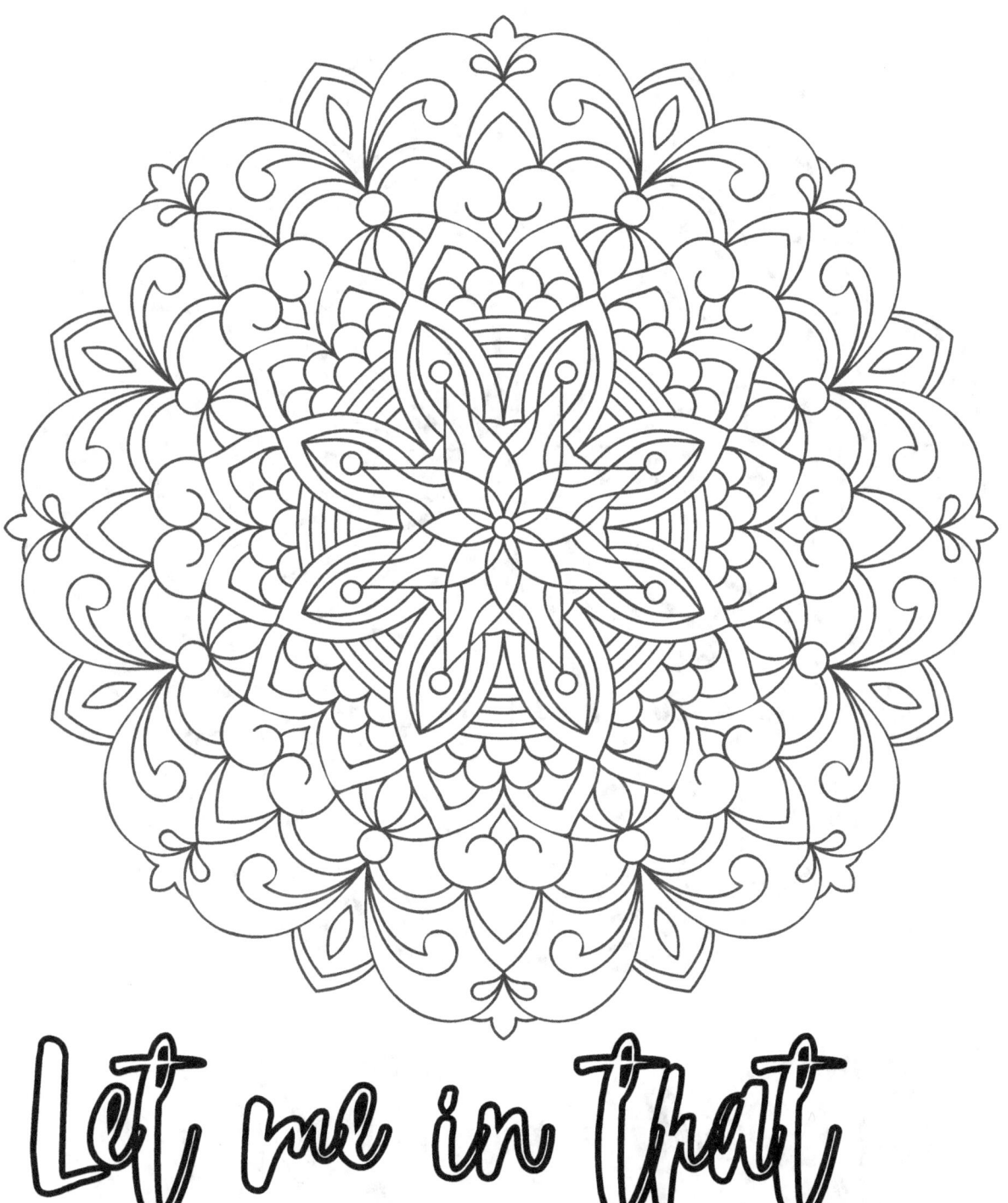

Let me in that butthole?

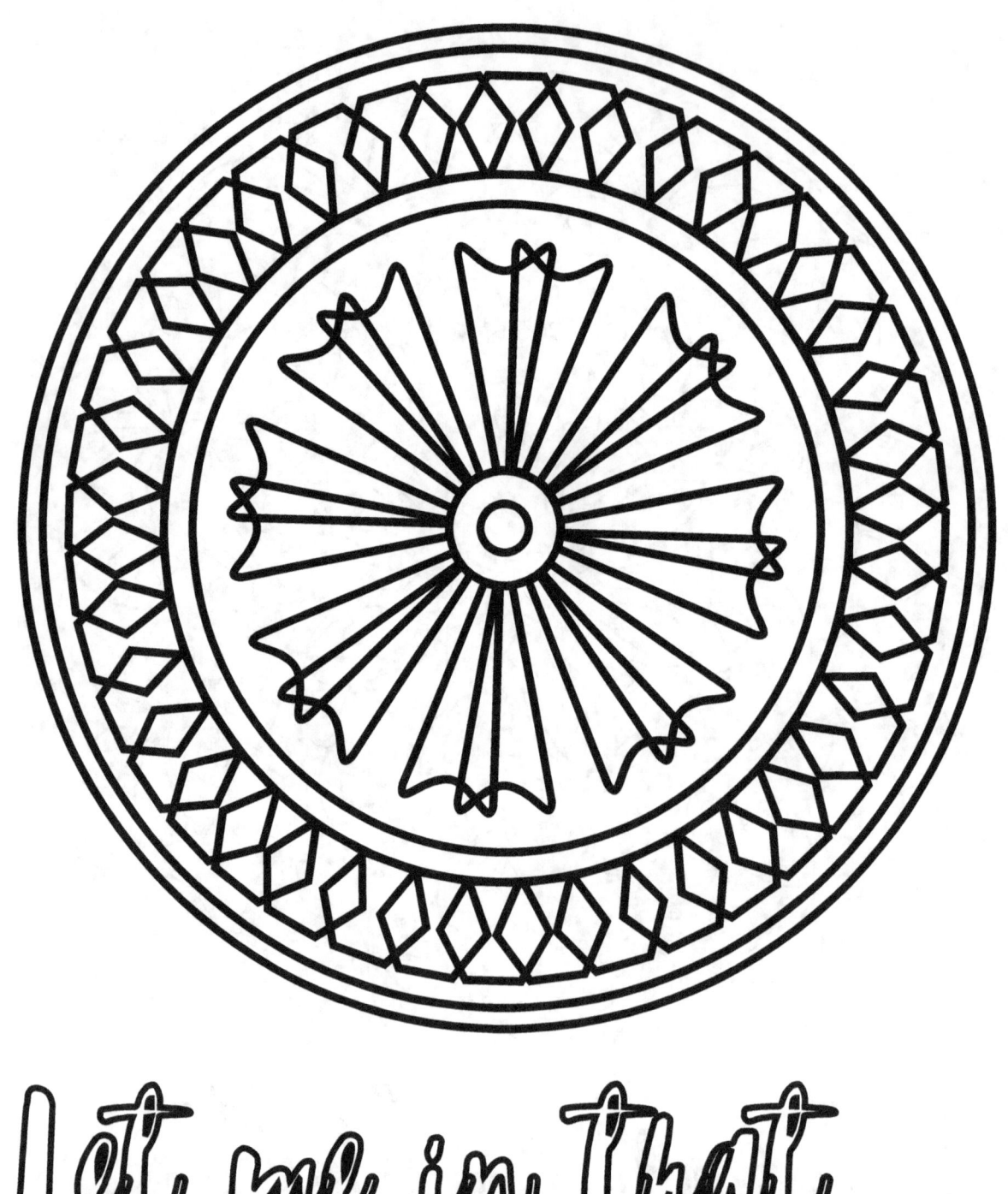

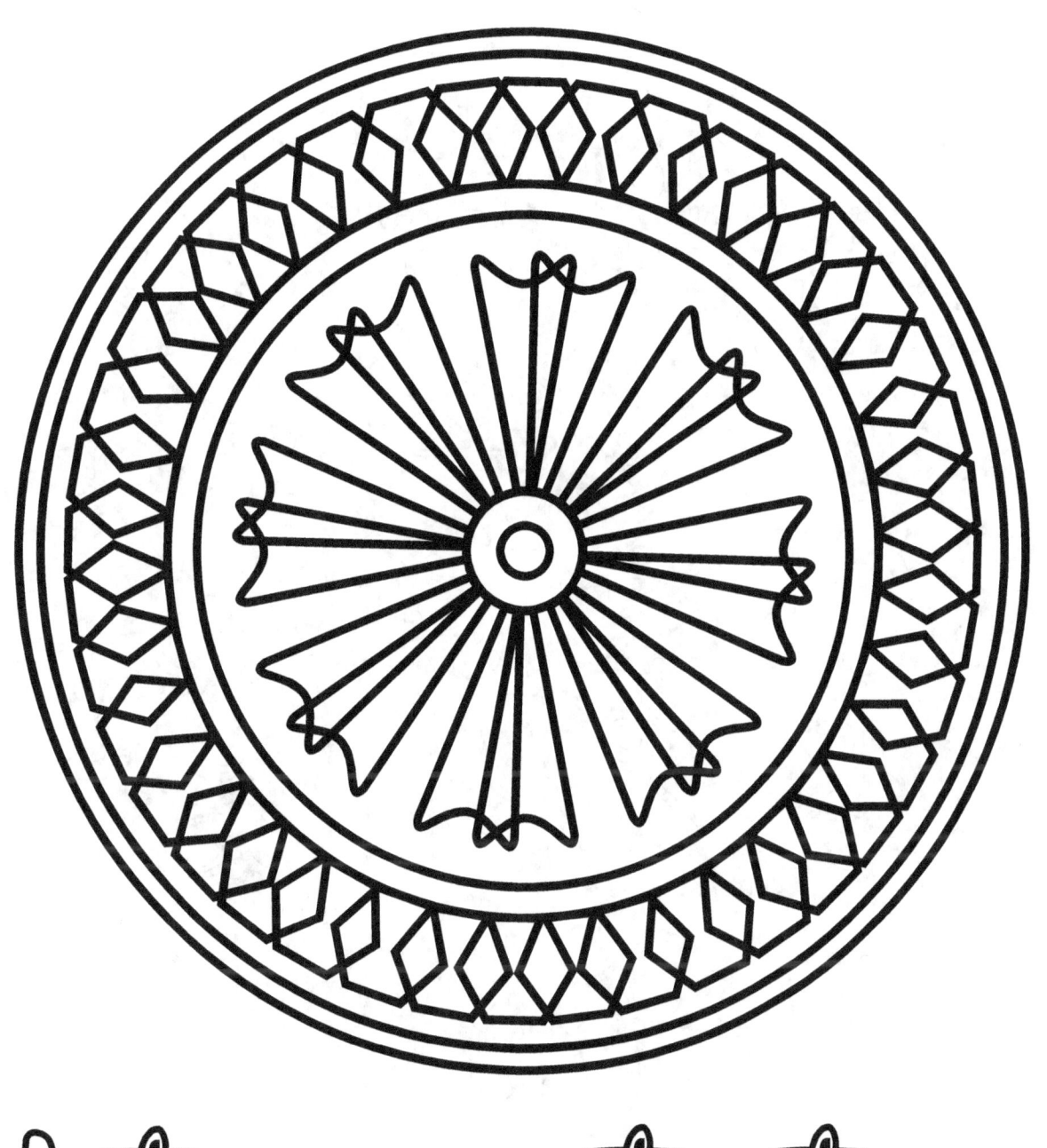

Let me in that butthole?

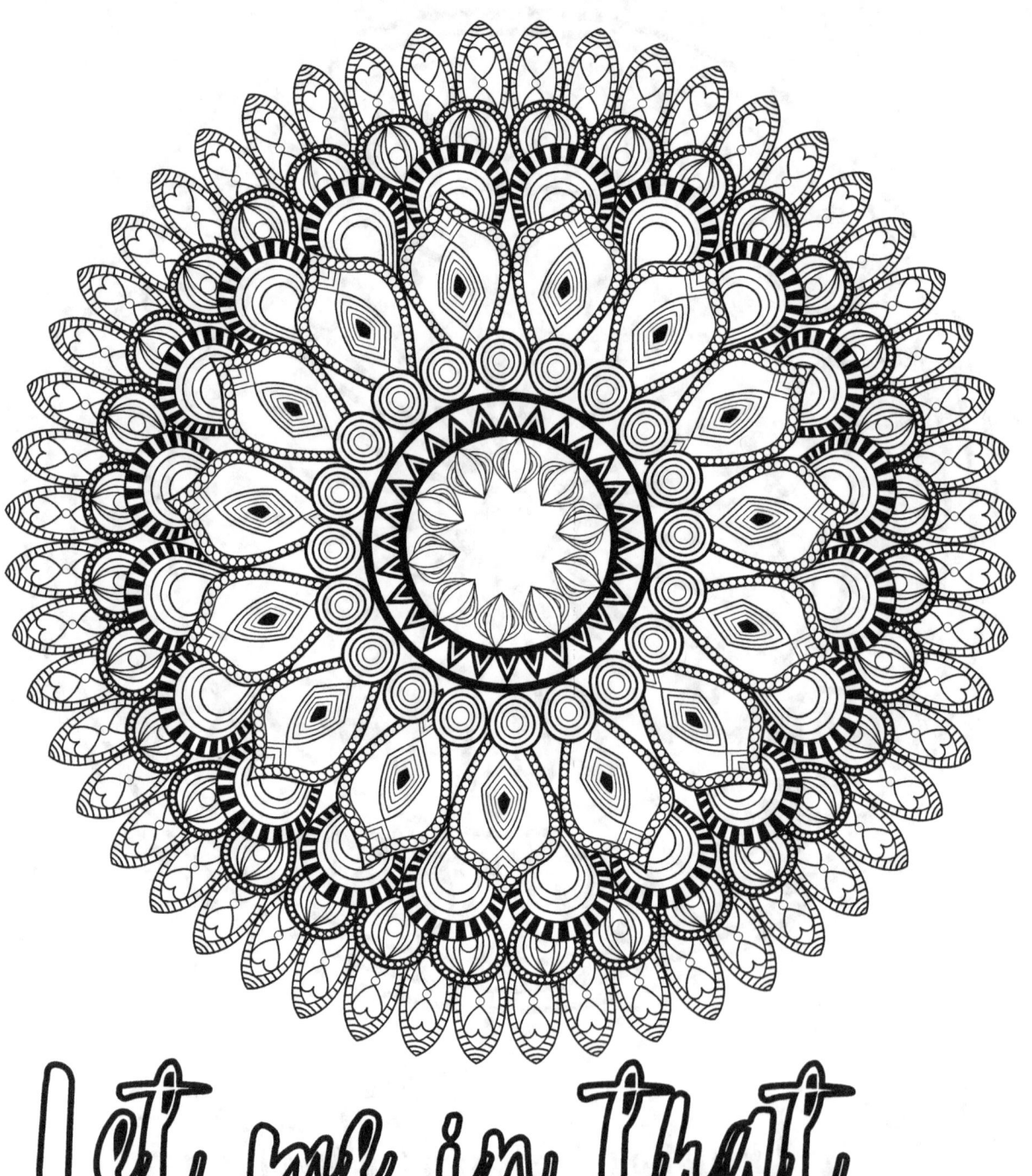

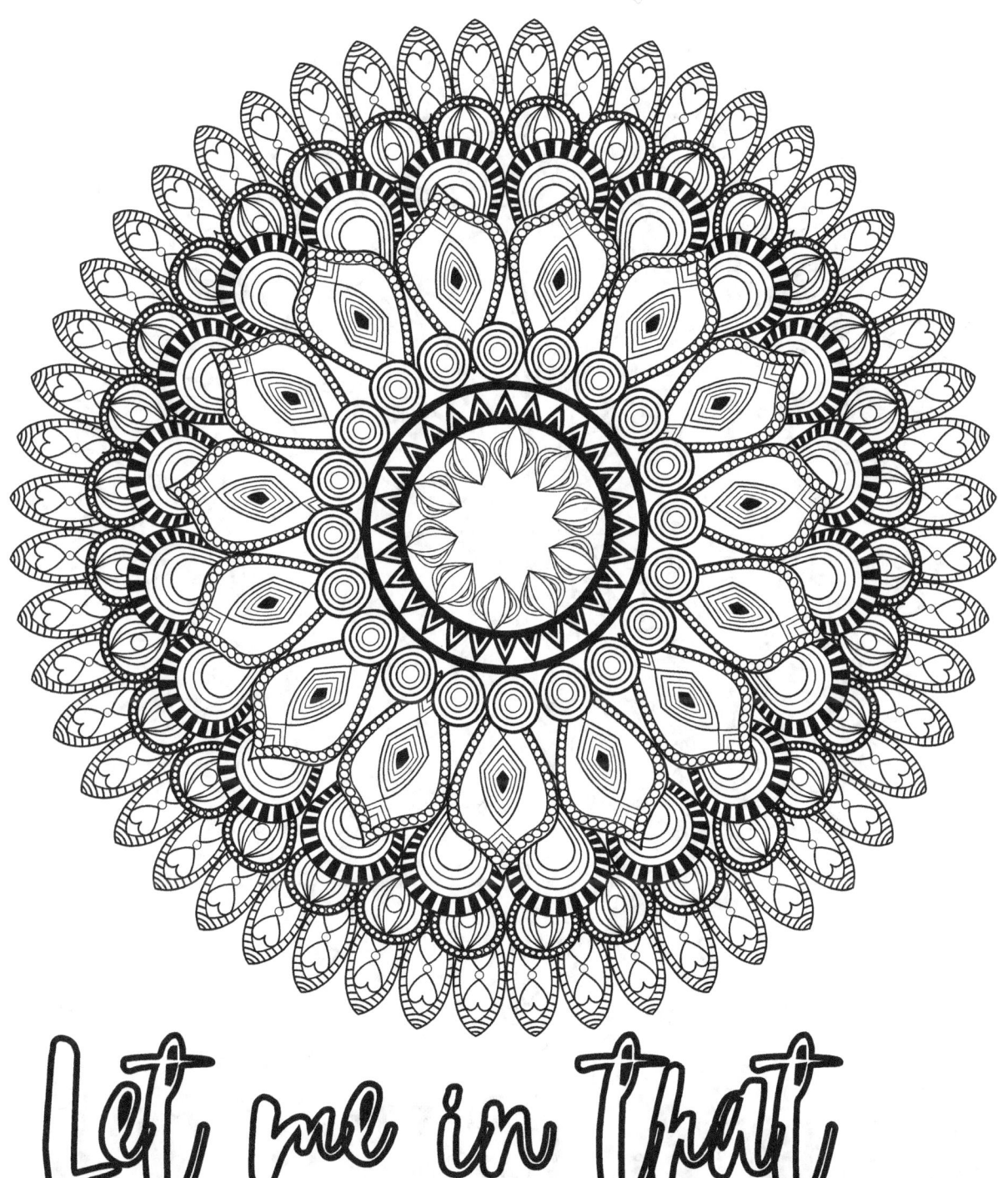

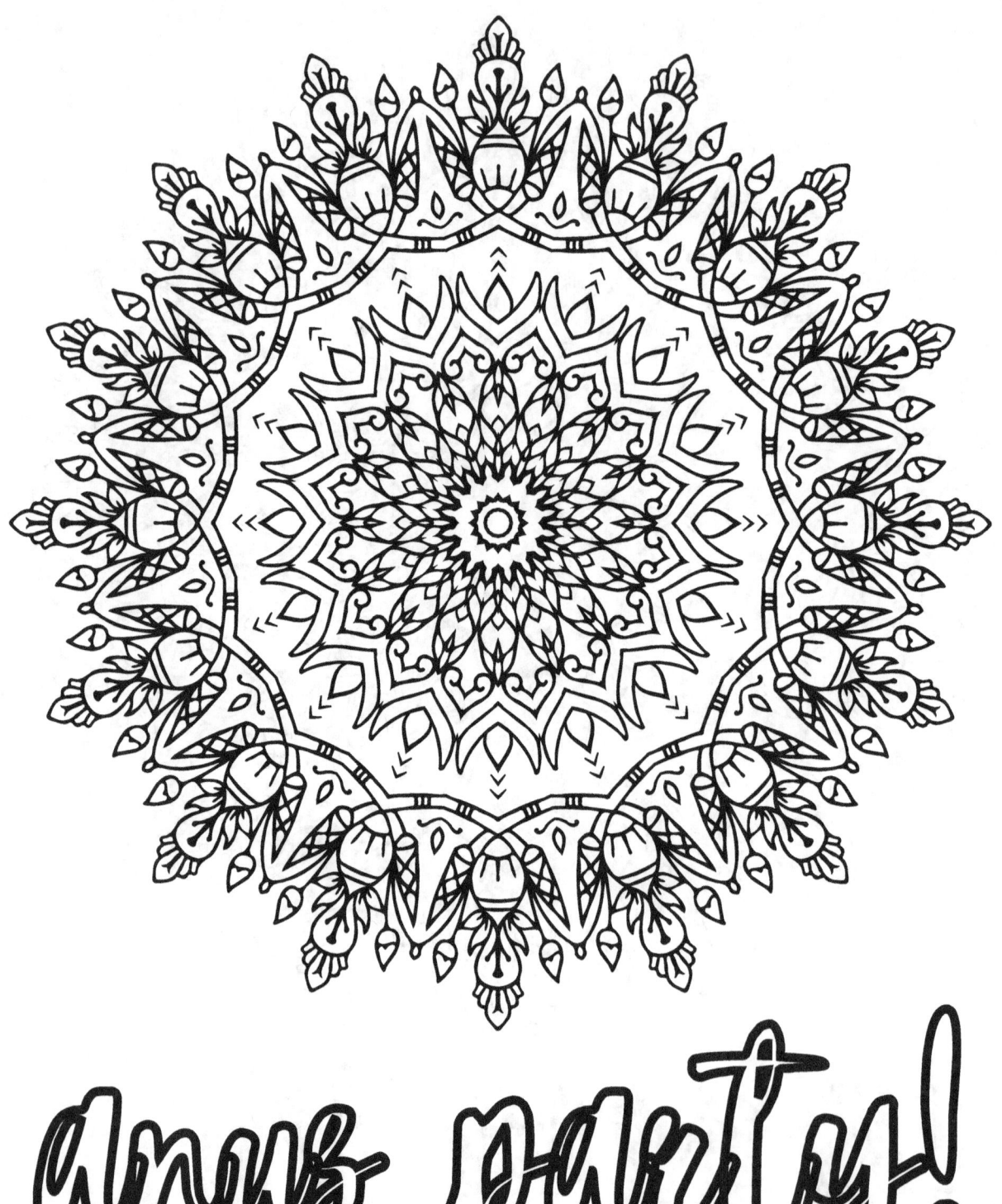

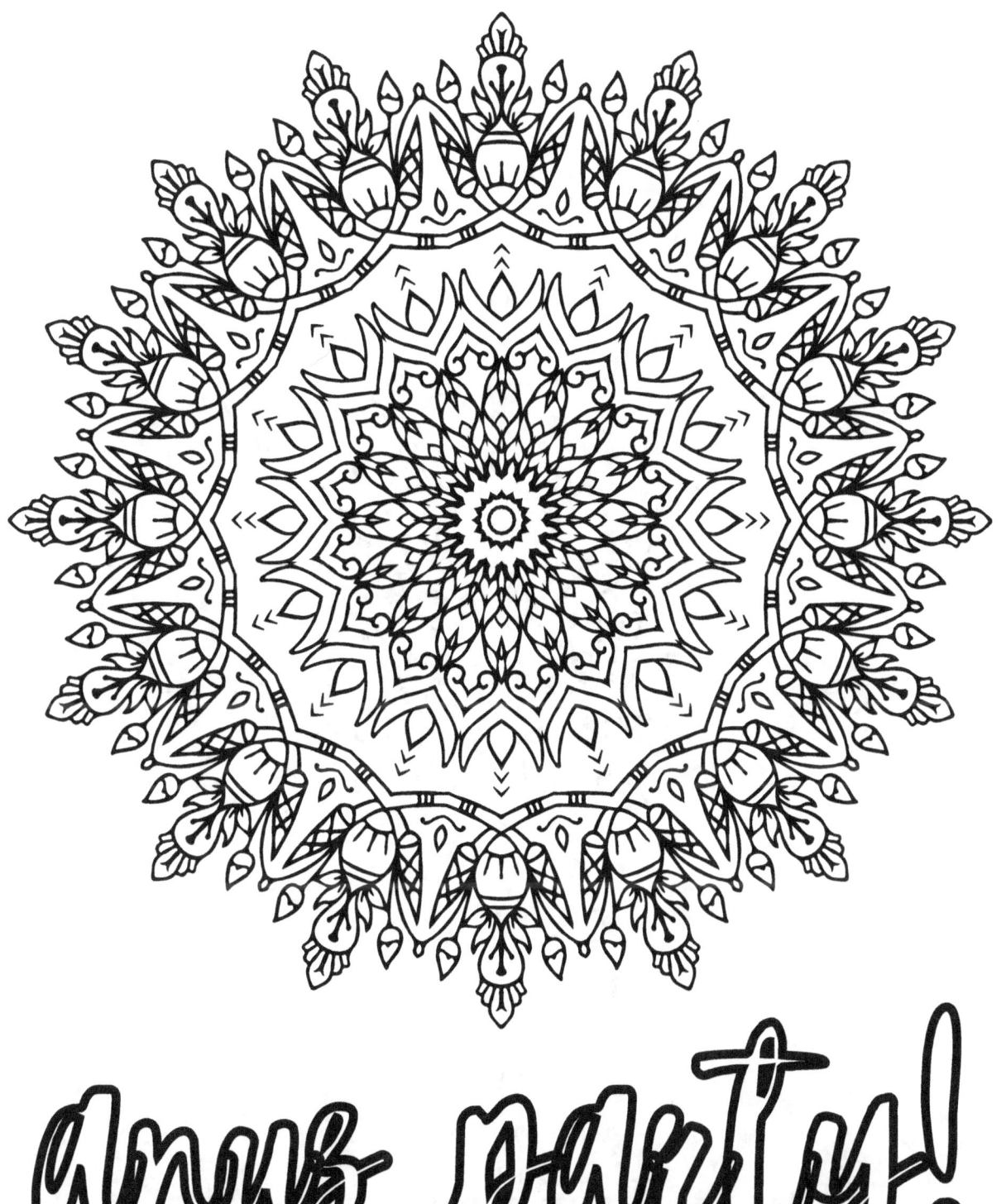

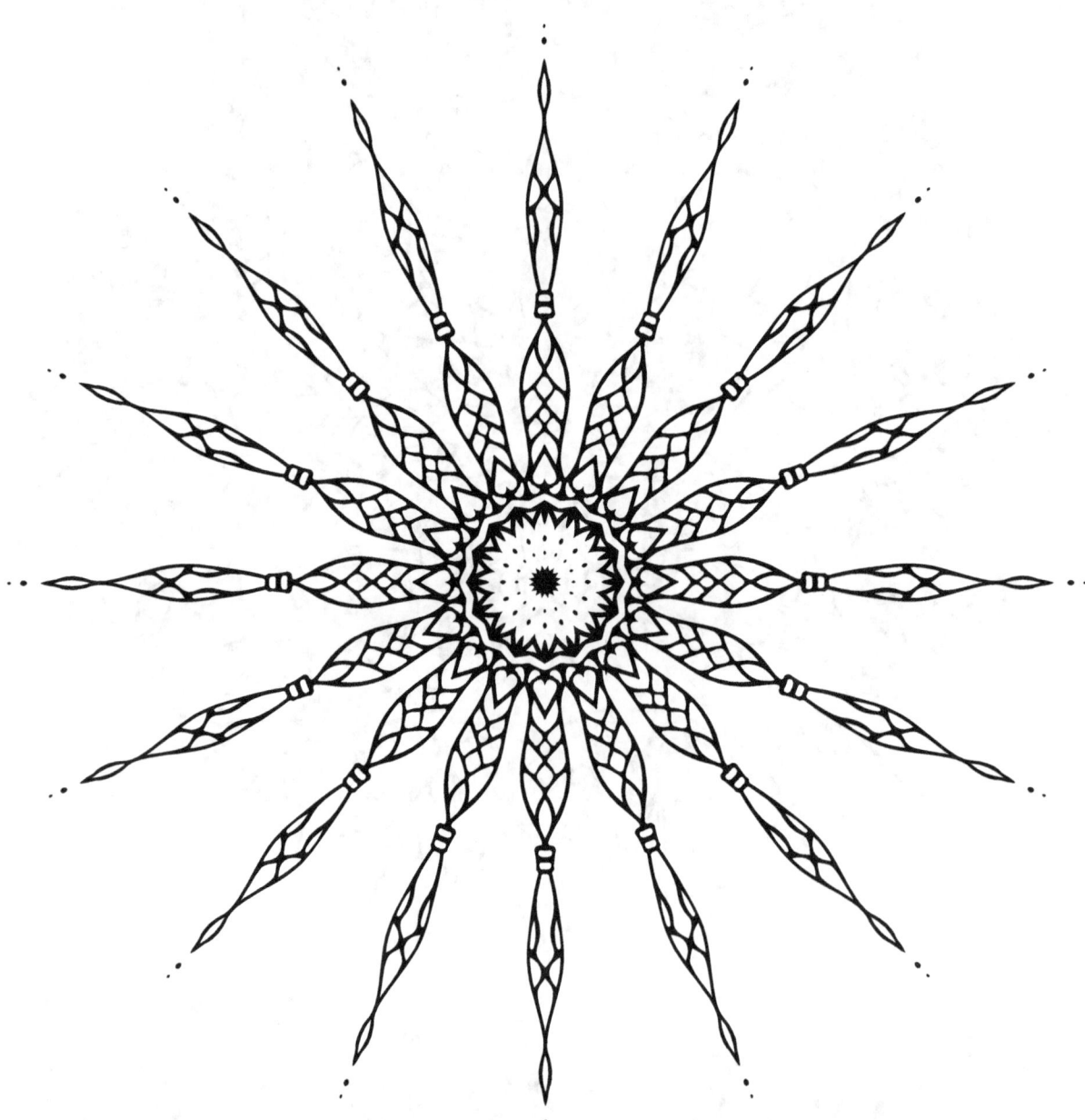

I'm talking about butt stuff, babe.

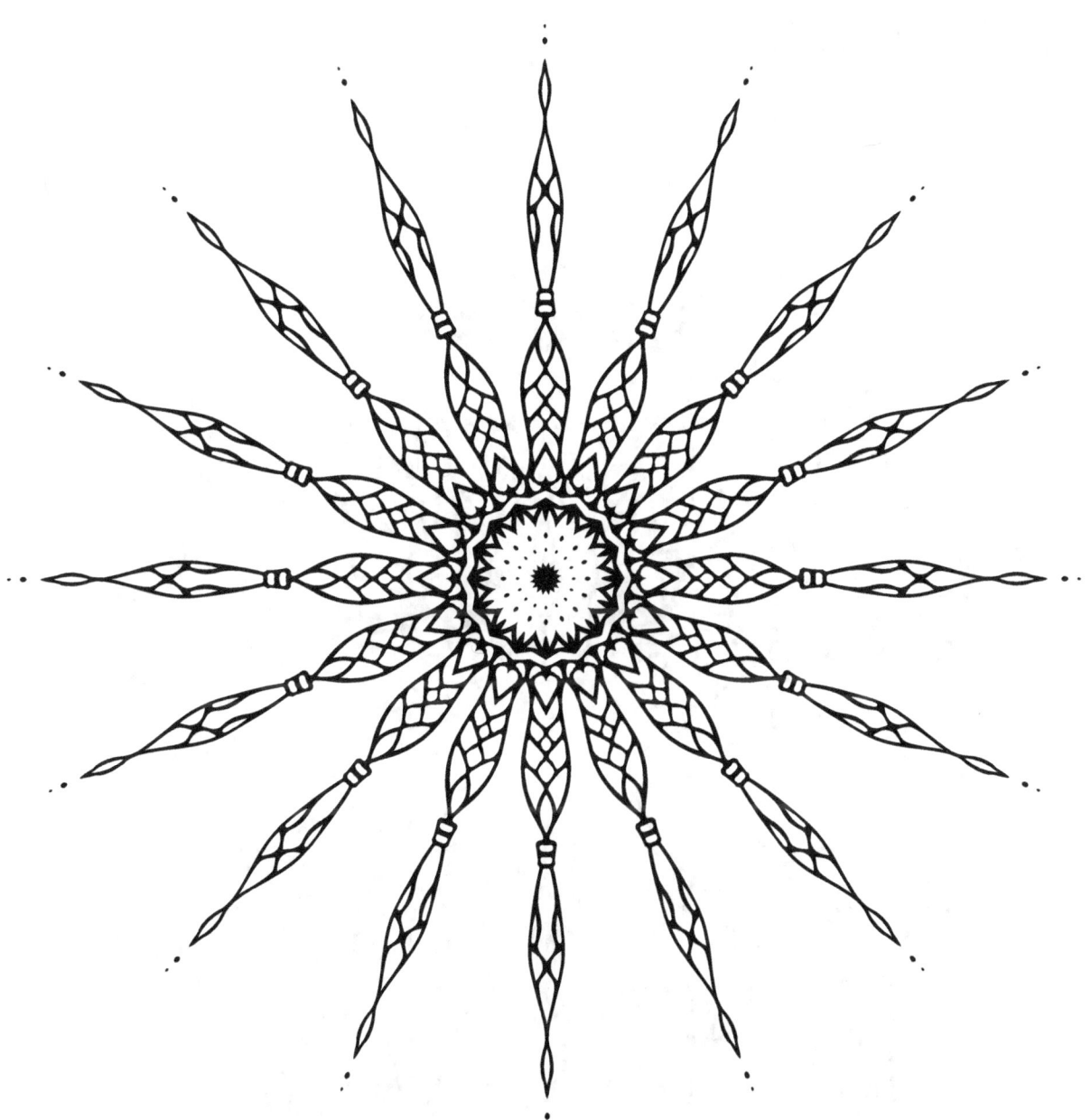

I'm talking about butt stuff, babe.

BUTT STUFF

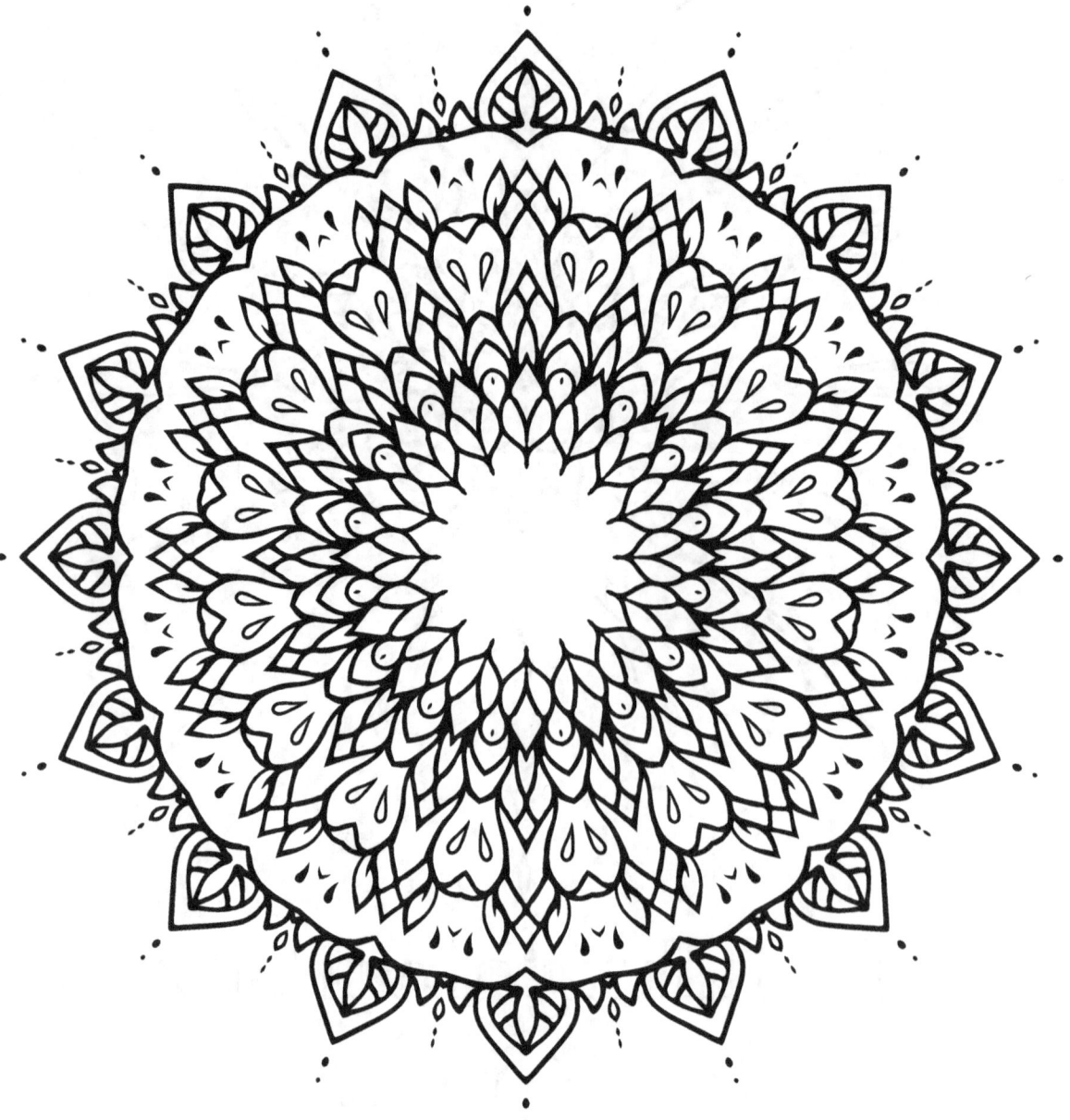

BUTT STUFF

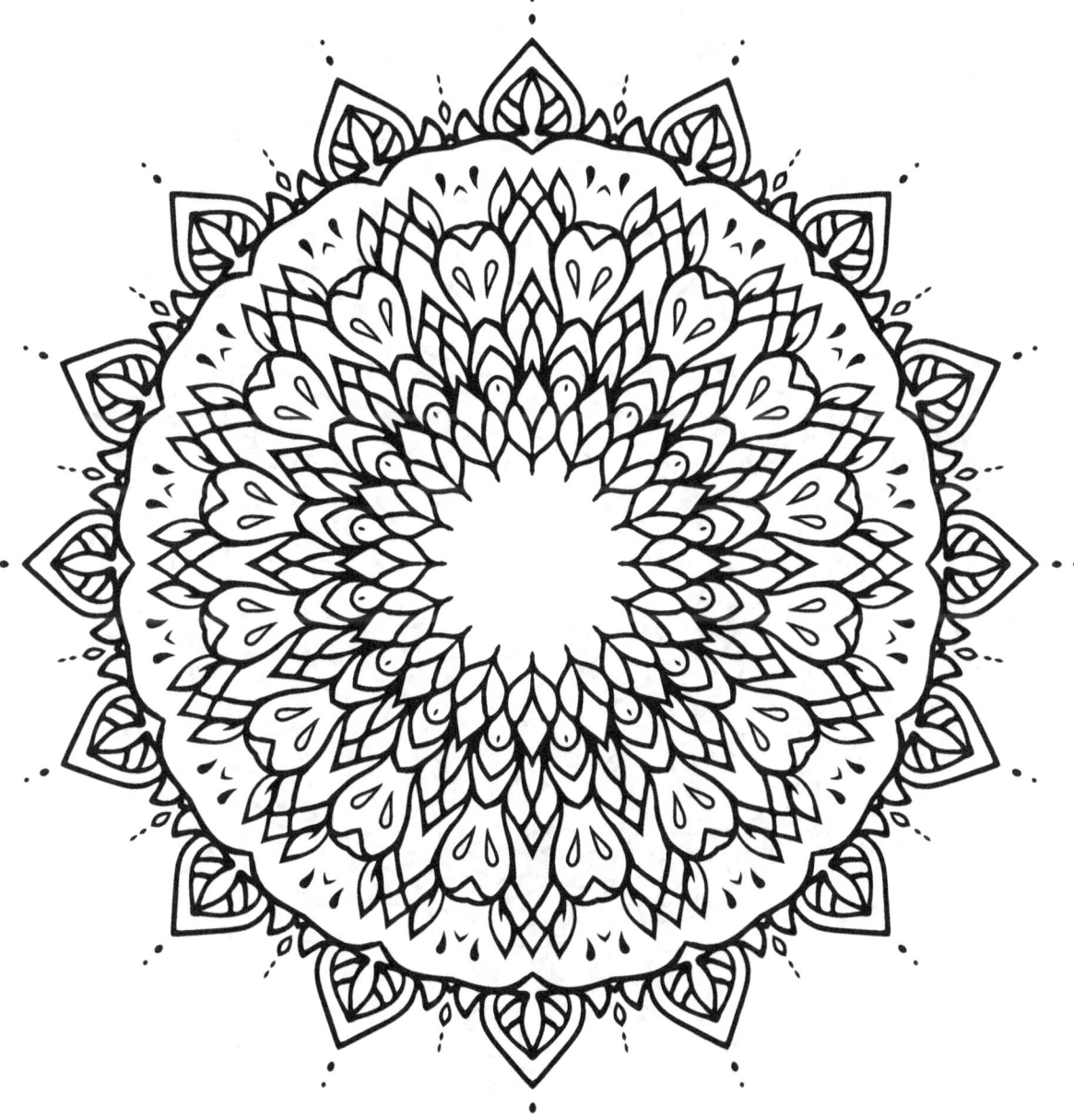

LET'S DO

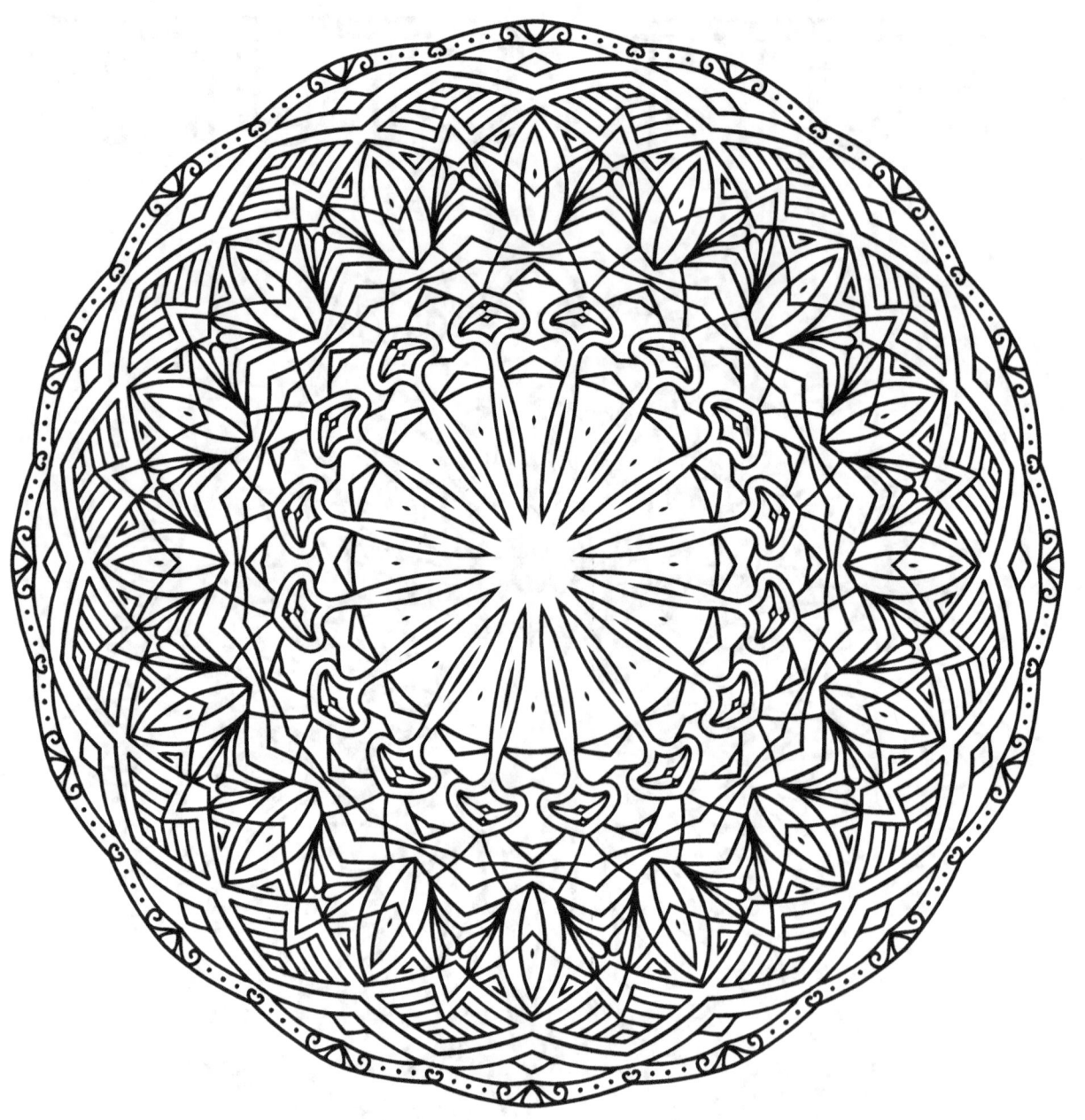

BUTT STUFF

LET'S DO

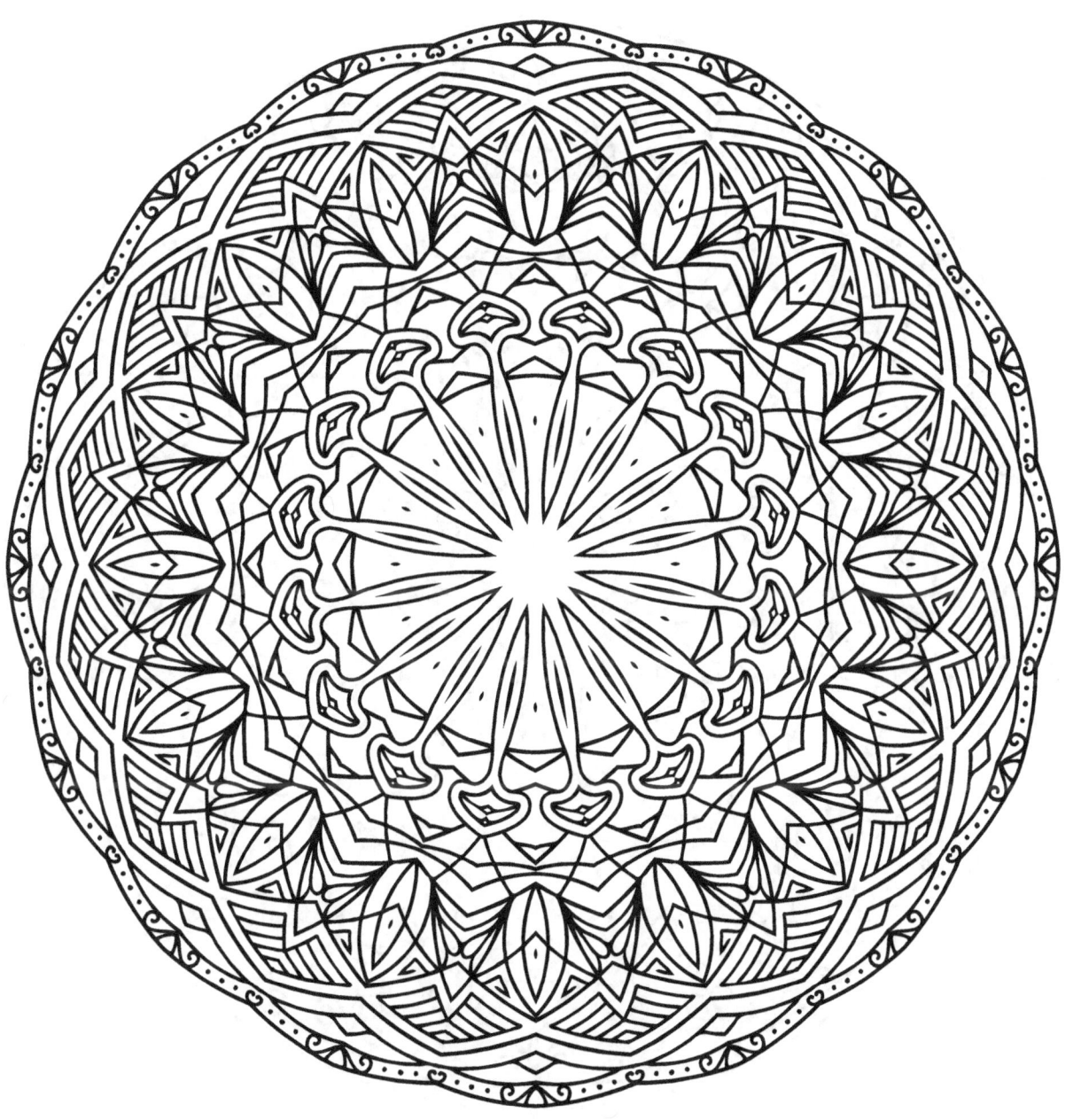

BUTT STUFF

DOING IT IN THE BUTT

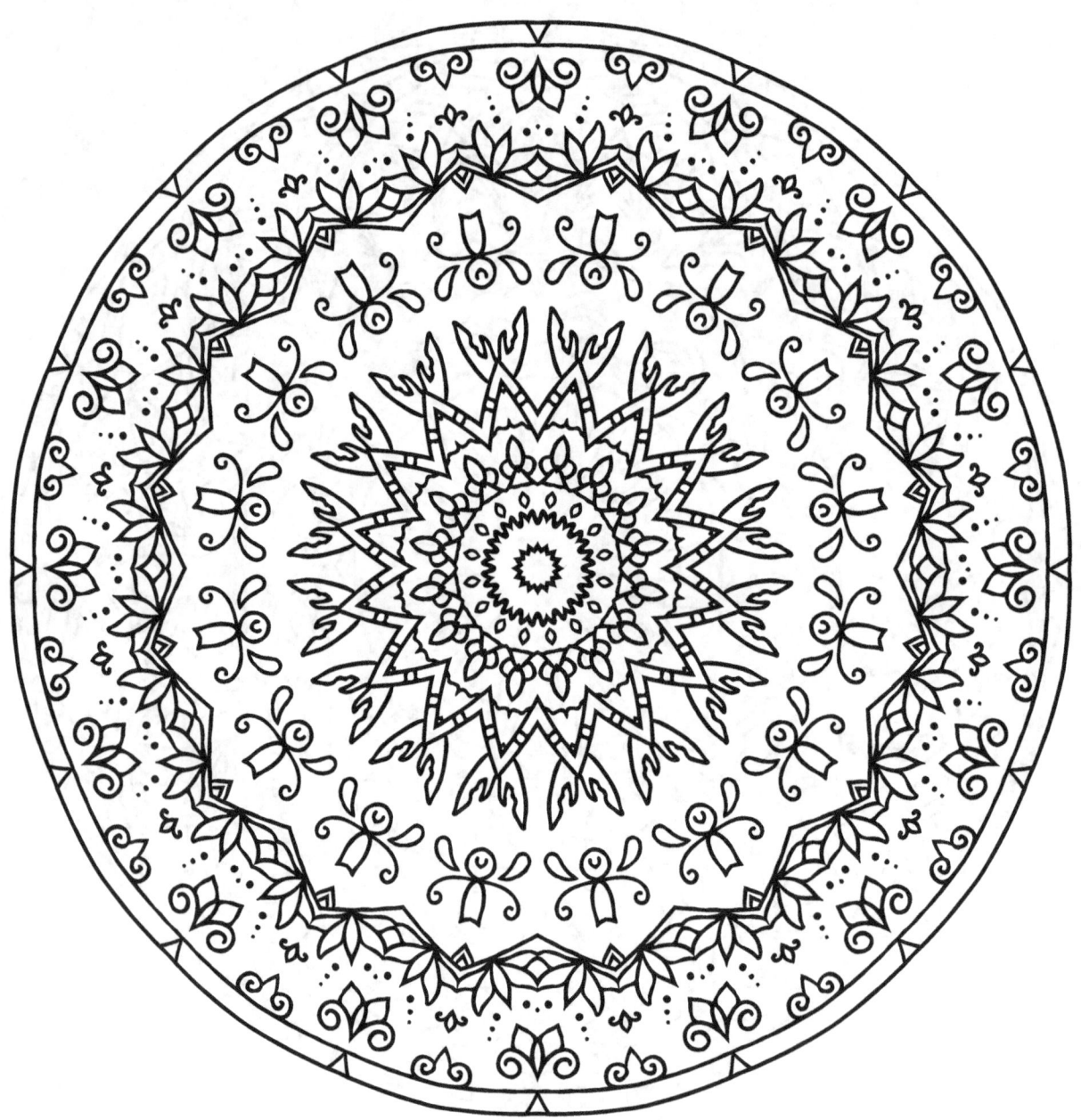

DOING IT IN THE BUTT

DOING IT IN THE BUTT

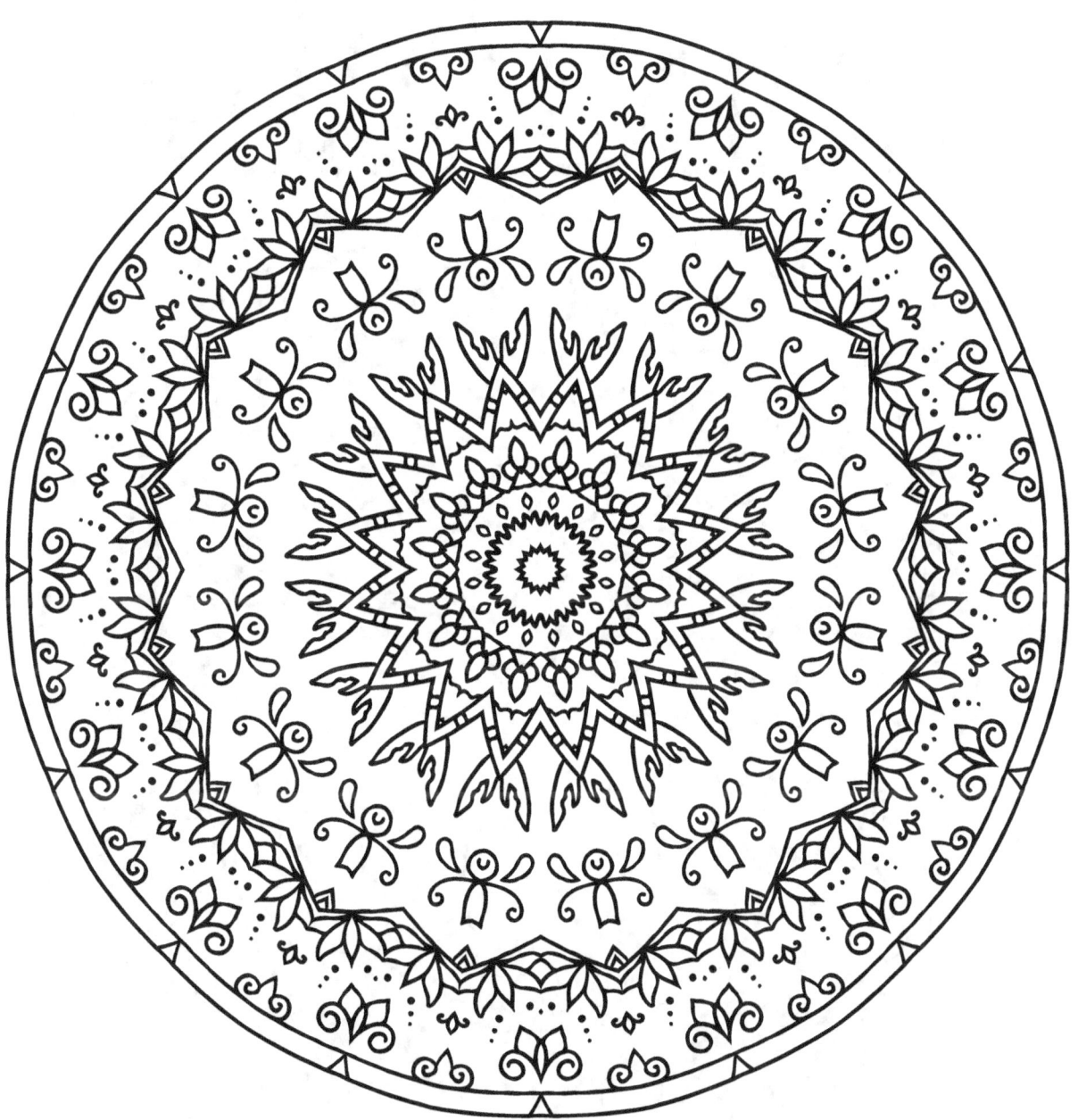

DOING IT IN THE BUTT

ANAL?

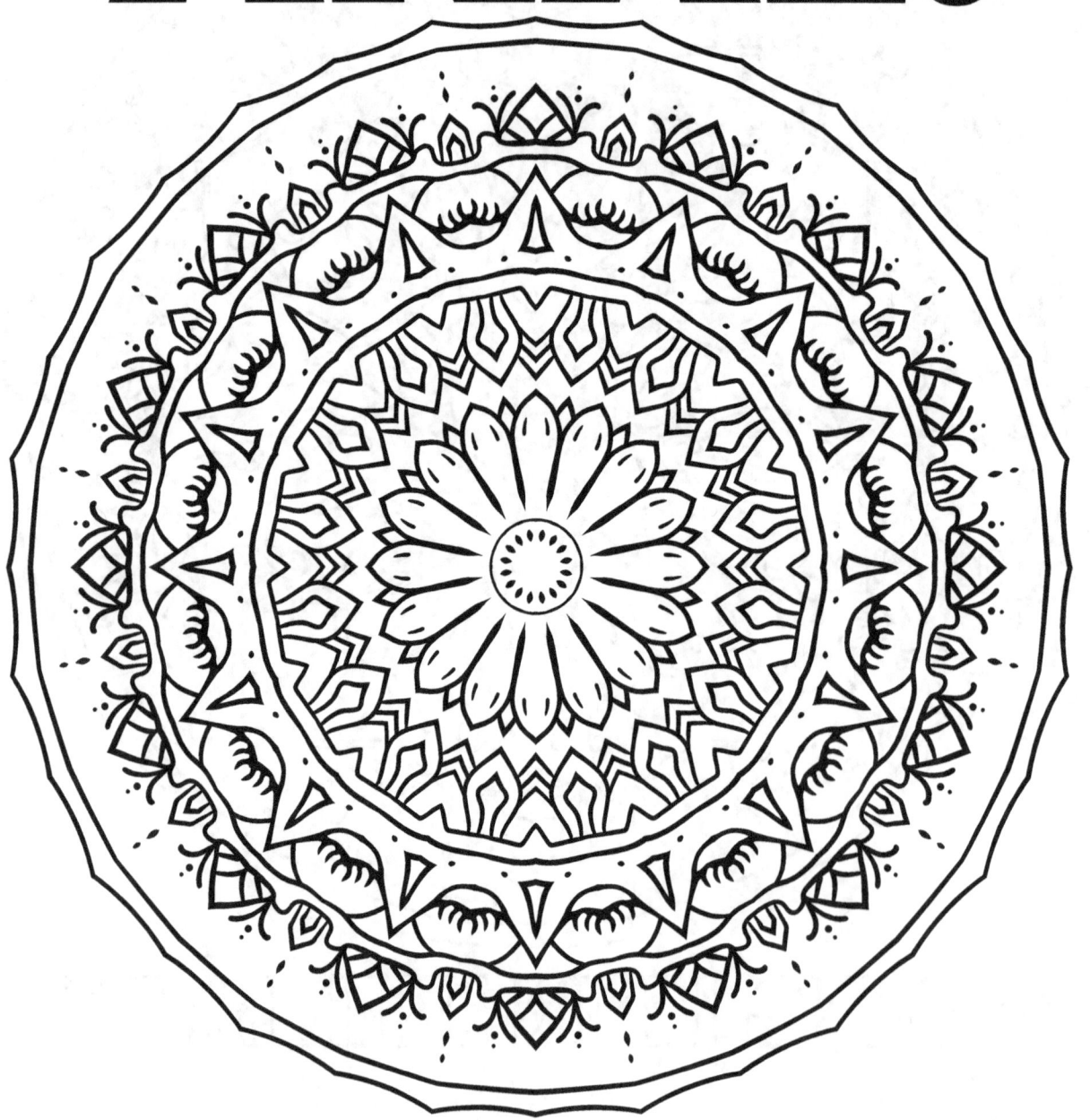

ANAL?

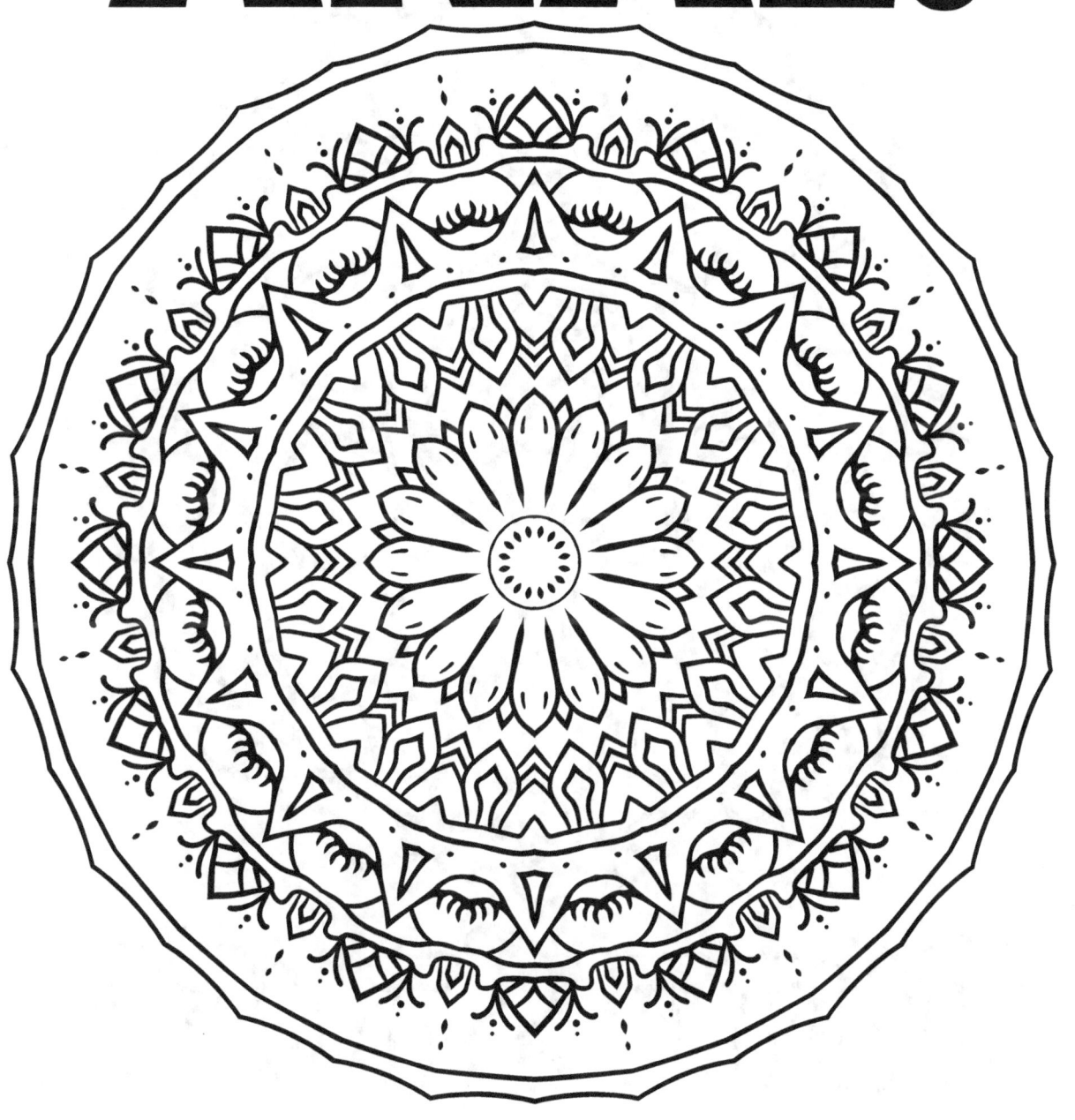

ME. YOU.

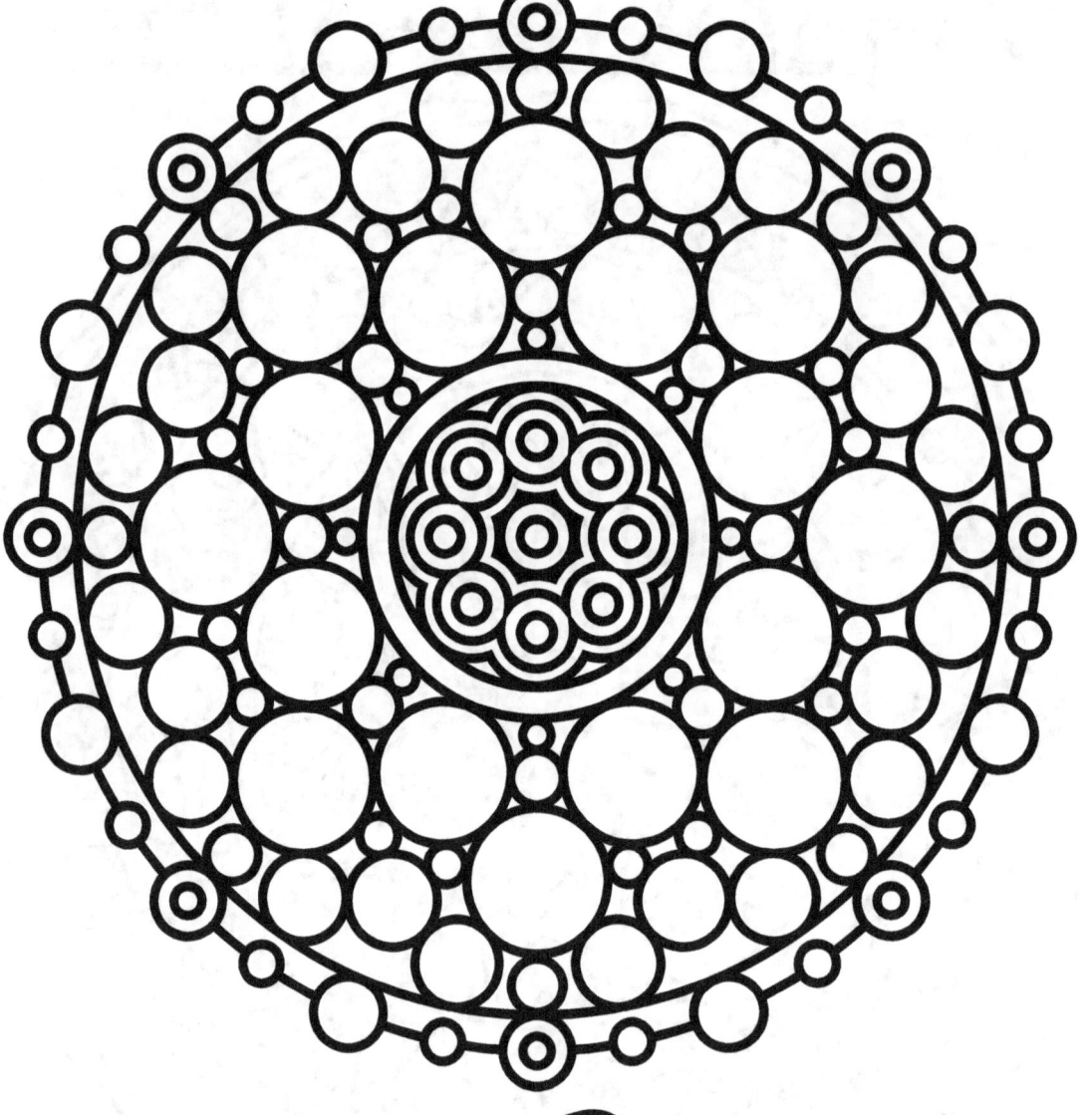

BUTT STUFF.

ME. YOU.

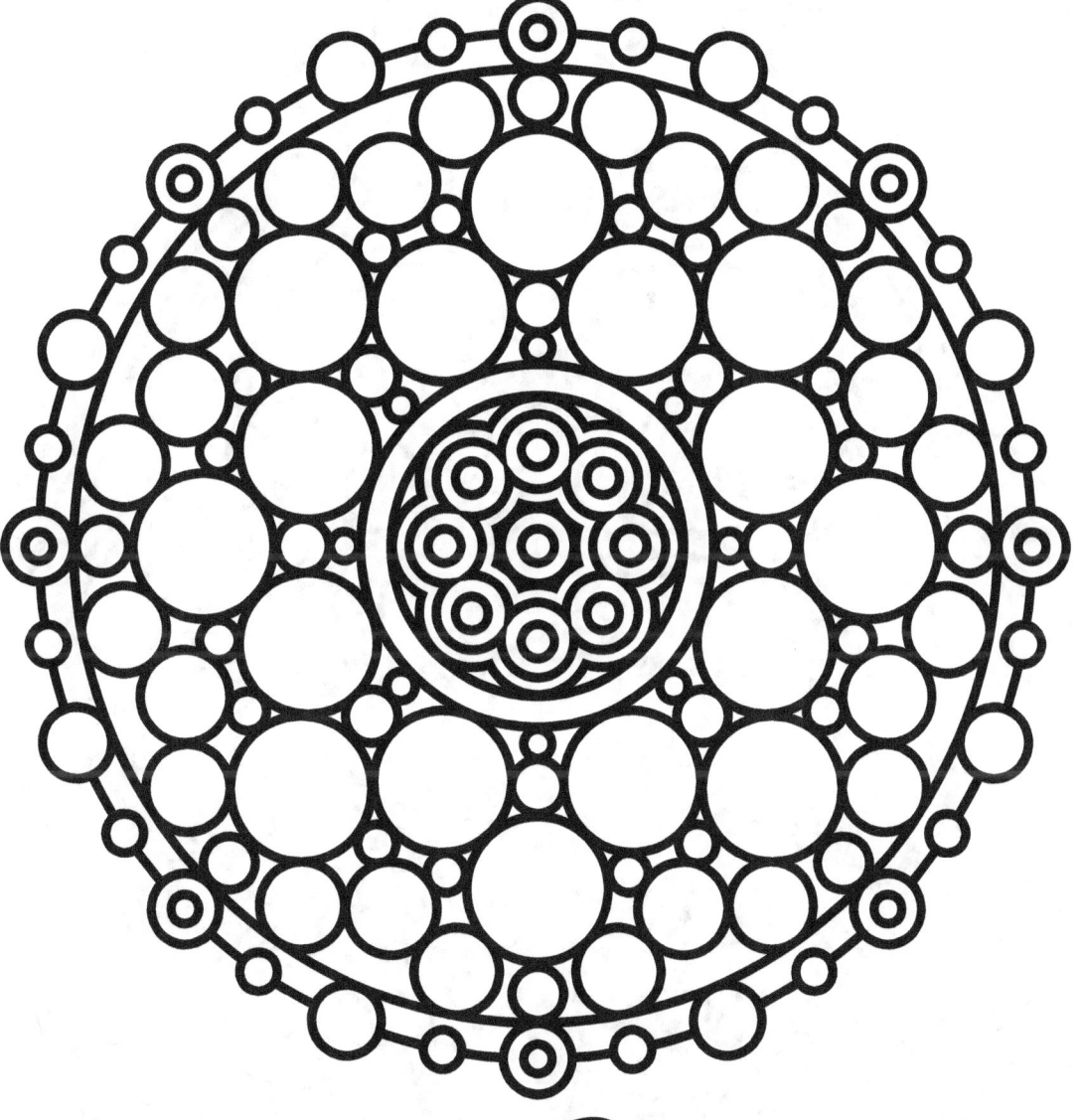

BUTT STUFF.

ANAL?

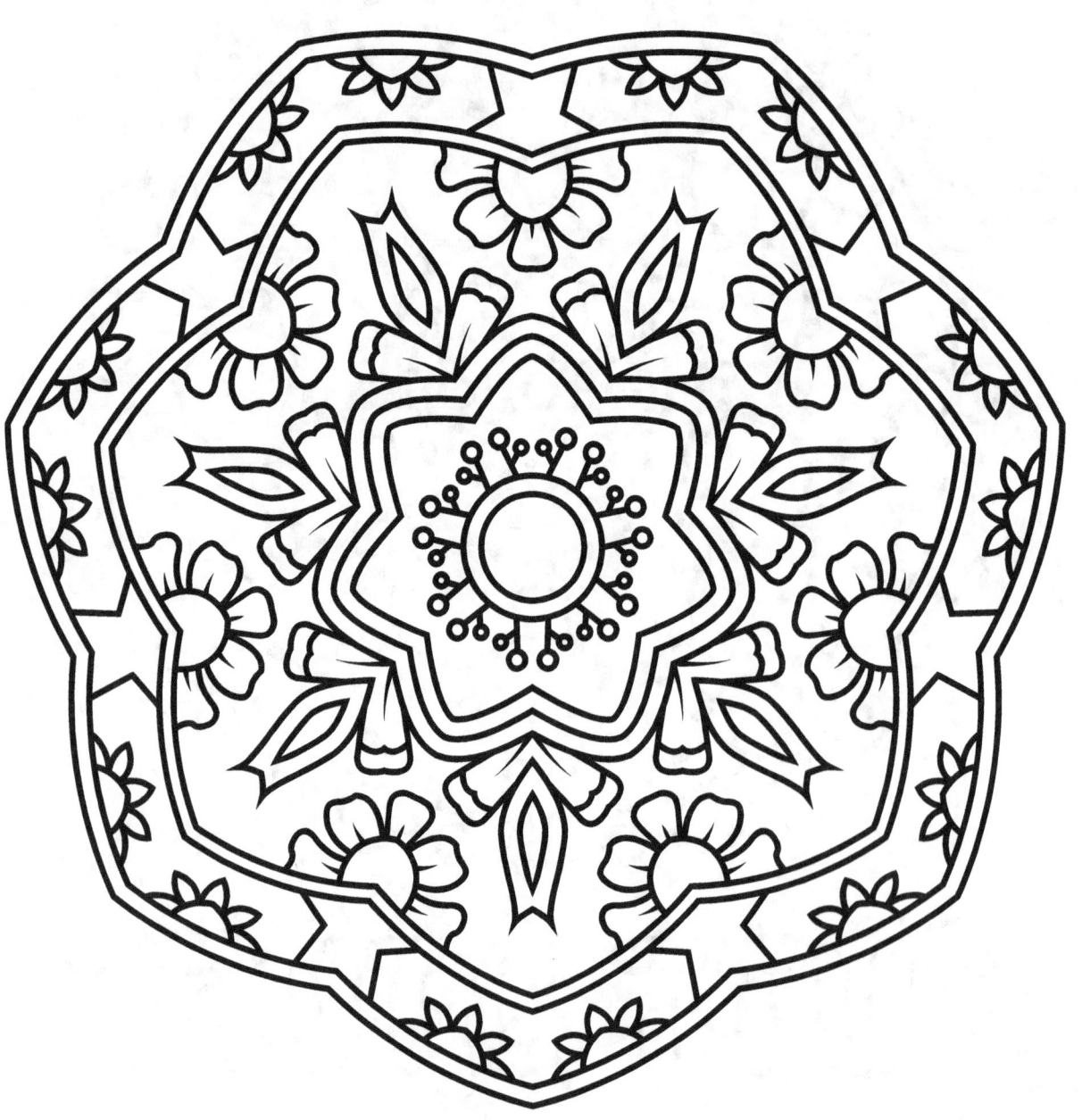

ANAL?

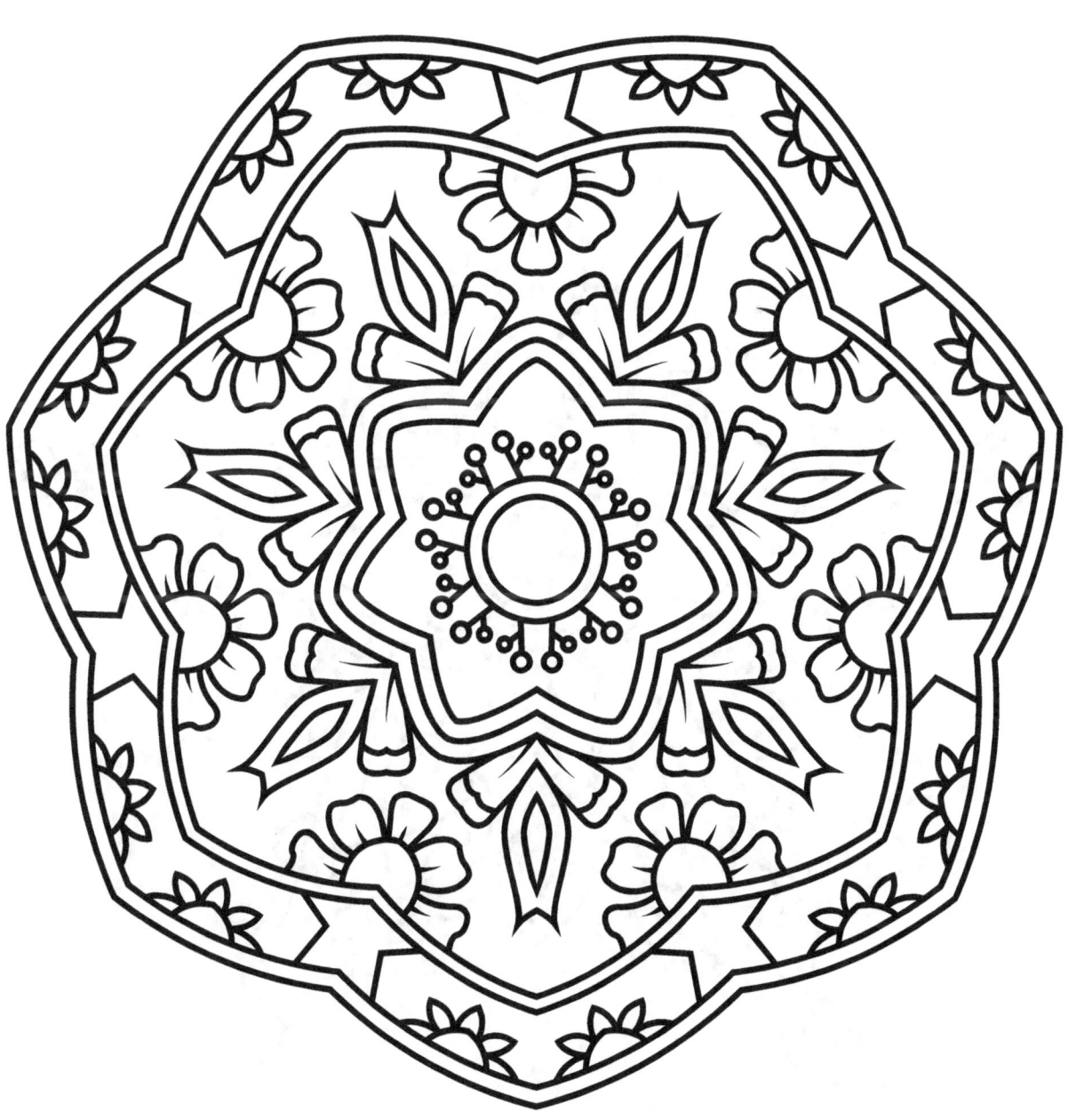

ANAL?

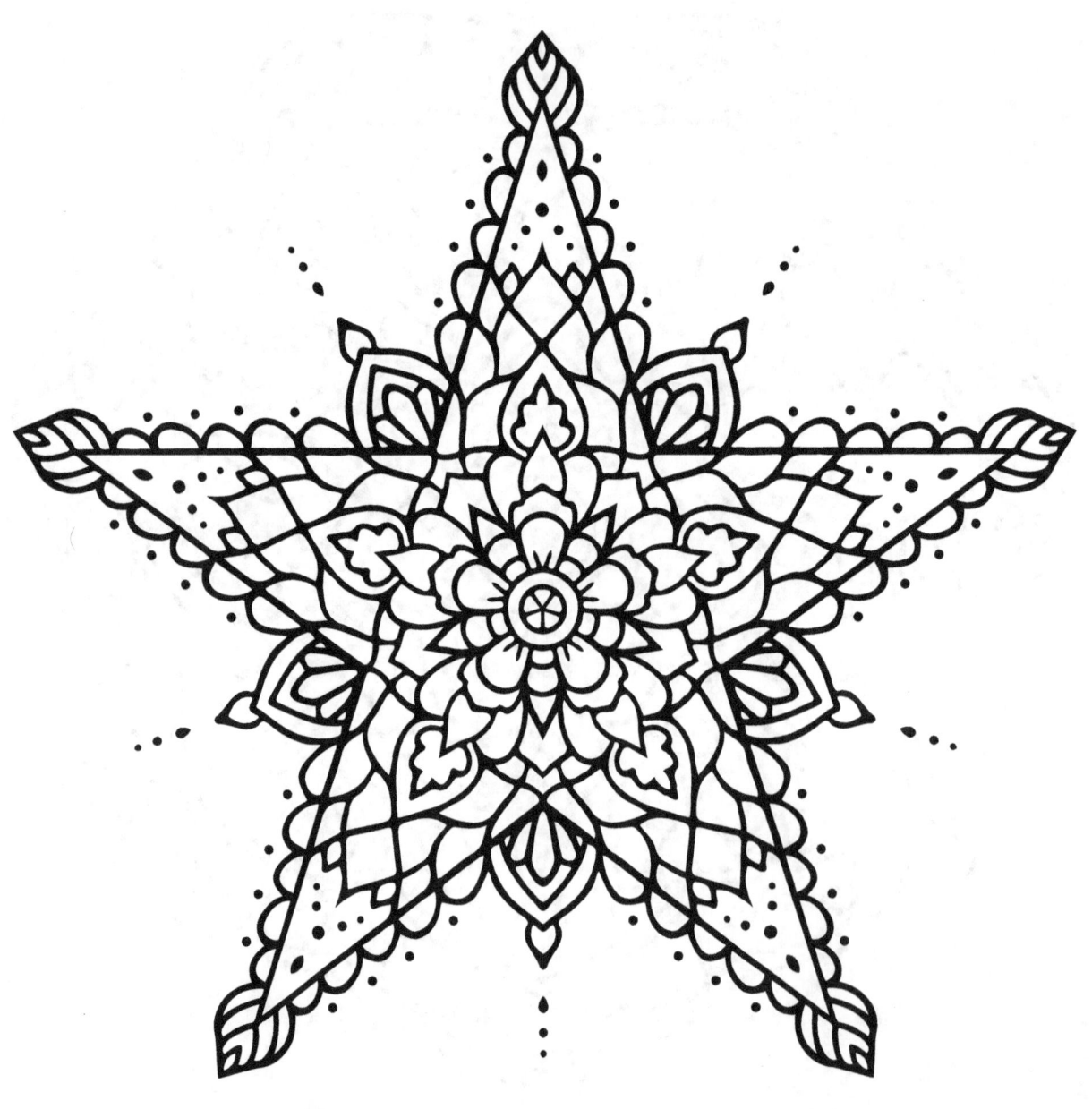